# PHUKET

WILLIAM BREDESEN

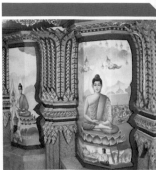

# Top 10 Phuket Highlights

# The Top 10 of Everything

# CONTENTS

## Phuket Area by Area

## Streetsmart

Within each Top 10 list in this book, no hierarchy of quality or popularity is implied. All 10 are, in the editor's opinion, of roughly equal merit.

Throughout this book, floors are referred to in accordance with American usage; i.e., the "first floor" is at ground level.

***Front cover and spine*** *Boat in Maya Bay, Ko Phi Phi Leh Island*
***Back cover*** *The ornate Wat Chalong in its landscaped gardens*
***Title page*** *The magnificent entrance to Phuket's Wat Chalong Buddhist temple*

# Welcome to
# Phuket

Luxurious, world-class resorts, mouthwatering cuisine, a vibrant nightlife, hidden islets and beaches, and ancient rainforests teeming with wildlife make this Thai island a tropical paradise. As well as leisure, the tranquil temples and multicultural shrines excite a voyage of discovery. With Eyewitness Top 10 Phuket, it is yours to explore.

There is truly something for everyone in Phuket. For relaxation, laze on lovely **Kata Beach** and snorkel with schools of multicolored fish; the adventurous should join the crowds in one of **Patong**'s bustling street markets and admire the 19th-century temple **Wat Chalong** or the entrancing Sino-Portuguese architecture of **Phuket Town**.

At 50 miles (80 km) long, Phuket (pronounced POO-get) is Thailand's largest island. However, it is also worth traveling beyond its shores to some of the easily accessible sights nearby. The karst cliffs and sea caves of **Phang Nga Bay** are rivaled by the surging waterfalls in the rainforests of **Khao Sok National Park**, north of Phuket. The nearby **Similan Islands** are rated among the world's top ten diving sites, and **Ko Phi Phi Don**, a short boat ride south of Phuket, offers a heady mix of raucous parties and silent, secluded beaches.

Whether you're visiting for a weekend or a week, our Top 10 guide brings together the best of everything Phuket and the surrounding areas have to offer, from the world-class resorts lining **Mai Khao Beach** to the pristine rainforests of **Khao Phra Thaeo Royal Forest and Wildlife Reserve**. The guide gives you useful tips throughout, from seeking out what's free to avoiding the crowds, alongside five easy-to-follow itineraries, designed to help you visit a clutch of sights in a short space of time. Add inspiring photography and detailed maps, and you've got the essential pocket-sized travel companion. **Enjoy the book, and enjoy Phuket.**

Clockwise from top: **Colorful boats at James Bond Island in Phang Nga Bay**; scuba diver in the Similan Islands; statue of the Buddha; stilt houses on Cheow Laan Lake; Chinese dragon carvings at Tha Rua shrine; junks in Phang Nga Bay; Sino-Portuguese buildings in Phuket

# Exploring Phuket

While it is tempting to find your perfect beach and just luxuriate there, Phuket offers an amazingly wide variety of treasures to discover. Beyond the beaches are rain forests, and the town of Phuket is an architectural and cultural jewel. To take in everything will require some form of private transport, but a good network of ferries serves the islands that surround Phuket. Here are two itineraries to help you make the most of your stay.

**Phang Nga Bay,** with its dramatic limestone pillars and aquatic grottoes, can be explored by Chinese junk cruise, kayaking expedition, or long-tailed boat.

**Key**
━ Two-day itinerary
━ Seven-day itinerary

To Khao Sok
National Park
Mai Khao Beach
Sirinat
National Park
Patong
Chal
Kata
Phromthep
Cape

## Two Days in Phuket

### Day ❶
**MORNING**
Explore the streets of old **Phuket Town** (see pp12–15), admiring the Sino-Portuguese architecture, and visit one of the atmospheric **Chinese shrines** (see pp46–7).
**AFTERNOON**
Head southwest from Phuket Town to **Wat Chalong** (see pp16–17), Phuket's most famous Buddhist temple. Drive to **Phromthep Cape** (see p48) and watch the sun set on the island's southern tip. Stay overnight at nearby **Kata** (see pp28–9) or **Patong** (see pp18–19) on the west coast.

### Day ❷
**MORNING**
Drive to **Sirinat National Park** (see pp22–3) and stroll along the quiet and undeveloped **Mai Khao Beach** (see p23). There are simple beachside seafood vendors here, perfect for lunch.

**AFTERNOON**
Head to **Khao Phra Thaeo Royal Forest and Wildlife Reserve** (see pp20–21) via routes 402 and 4127. Trek to **Ton Sai Waterfall** for a swim, then visit the **Gibbon Rehabilitation Project**. Have dinner in Phuket Town.

## Seven Days in Phuket

### Day ❶
Follow the morning's plan for Day 1 of the Phuket itinerary, taking in the sights of historic old Phuket Town. After lunch, take a taxi to Rassada Port, then board a ferry to Ko Yao Noi in **Phang Nga Bay** (see pp36–7). Spend your first night here.

### Day ❷
Take a boat tour of the dramatic limestone stacks and mangrove forests of the bay, then visit the amazing sea caves on a kayaking expedition in the evening. Spend a second night at Ko Yao Noi.

Around Phuket

Khao Sok
National Park

Khao Lak

Similan
Islands
National
Park

Phang Nga
Bay

Ko Yao
Noi

See Phuket
map, left

Mai
Khao

Phuket
Town

Ko Phi
Phi Don

Ko Phi Phi
Leh

0 km    25
0 miles   25

Gibbon
Rehabilitation
Project

Khao Phra Thaeo
Royal Forest and
Wildlife Reserve

Sai
terfall

huket

Phuket
Town

Rassada
Port

To Ko Yao Noi

0 km    5
0 miles   5

## Day ❸
Take a boat from Ko Yao Noi to **Ko Phi Phi Don** (see p101) to spend a night there. Enjoy the views from the **Phi Phi Viewpoint** (see p99), then leave the busy Tonsai area and follow the coast to one of the more secluded bays. Take a sunset cruise to spectacular **Maya Bay** (see p100) – the very image of a perfect beach – on **Ko Phi Phi Leh** (see p48). This islet is uninhabited, but has been the set for several Hollywood movies.

## Day ❹
Make your way back to Phuket by speedboat or ferry, and then follow the afternoon's plan for Day 1 of the Phuket itinerary.

## Day ❺
Follow the program for Day 2 of the Phuket itinerary, but spend the night at Mai Khao Beach.

## Day ❻
Spend the day kayaking or trekking in **Khao Sok National Park** (see pp32–5). This pristine rainforest environment includes spectacular limestone cliffs and a wide variety

of flora and fauna. Stay overnight in the coastal town of **Khao Lak** (see p100). This is mainly a jumping off place for dive trips to the islands, but Nang Tong beach, just south of town, is lovely and quiet.

## Day ❼
Take a boat tour to the **Similan Islands National Park** (see pp30–31), 50 miles (80 km) from Khao Lak. Both the scuba diving and snorkeling here are superb. Note that the islands are closed from mid-May to mid-October due to poor weather.

**Phi Phi Viewpoint** on Phi Phi Don offers views over two magnificent bays, Loh Dalum and Tonsai.

# Top 10 Phuket Highlights

Ko Tapu karst formation at James Bond Island, Phang Nga Bay

# TOP 10 Phuket Highlights

Phuket's extraordinary tropical setting needs little introduction. The marvelous white-sand beaches, rolling green hills, and crystal-clear waters have lured visitors for centuries. But the island boasts more than sublime beaches. Phuket and its environs are also home to a multitude of cultural highlights.

### Phuket Town ①
Magnificent architecture, Chinese shrines, bustling outdoor marketplaces, and authentic local cuisine are all found in Phuket's cultural heart (see pp12–15).

### ② Wat Chalong
Phuket's most important Buddhist temple is lavish with sacred sculptures and imagery. The Grand Pagoda houses a bone fragment of the Buddha himself (see pp16–17).

### Patong ③
Wild and uninhibited, Patong is the island's busiest tourist beach. Home to countless hotels, restaurants, and nightclubs, this is the ideal spot for people who want to be in the middle of the action (see pp18–19).

### ④ Khao Phra Thaeo Royal Forest and Wildlife Reserve
With jungle trails, waterfalls, and many exotic animals and plants, this national park features a wealth of wild attractions (see pp20–21).

### Sirinat National Park ⑤
On Phuket's pristine northwest coast, Sirinat National Park grants protection to a large area of undeveloped beachfront, as well as the island's last surviving mangrove forest. A number of upscale hotels are located here (see pp22–3).

Suan Maphrao

Phuket

Sirinat National Park ⑤

Sakoo

Nai Thon

Bang Tao Bay

Cherngtalay

Kamala Bay · Kama

Patong ③

Karon

Kata Beach ⑦

Naiharn Beach ⑥

Around Phuket

Khao Sok National Park ⑨
Takua Pa
Thap Lamu
⑧ Similan Islands National Park
Phang Nga
Andaman Sea
Kok Loi
⑩ Phang Nga Bay
Phuket
Phuket Town

0 km 30
0 miles 30

Kung Bay
Muang Mai
6012
4027
Bang Rong
④ Khao Phra Thaeo Royal Forest and Wildlife Reserve
halang
Na Sat
4025
Tha Rua
Sapam Bay
athu
4024
Ratsada
402
① Phuket Town
② Wat Chalong
Ao Makham
4021
Ao Chalong
Chalong Bay
awai

0 km 5
0 miles 5

### ⑥ Naiharn Beach
At Phuket's southern tip, this idyllic beach provides one of the island's loveliest tropical backdrops. Phromthep Cape offers breathtaking sunset views *(see pp26–7)*.

### ⑦ Kata Beach
Once a hippie haven, Kata is now home to upscale resorts, and is a favorite with couples and families. The gorgeous beach and clear turquoise waters are highlights *(see pp28–9)*.

### Similan Islands National Park ⑧
The waters surrounding the Similans provide incredible visibility, ideal for viewing exotic marine life and dramatic underwater rock formations and reefs. This is one of the world's top diving destinations *(see pp30–31)*.

### ⑨ Khao Sok National Park
At the heart of this park are ancient evergreen forests, majestic limestone peaks, and Cheow Laan Lake, with its floating bamboo-raft houses *(see pp32–5)*.

### Phang Nga Bay ⑩
Stunning limestone cliffs jut up from this bay, where world-famous sights include James Bond Island and the magnificent Ko Phi Phi. Kayakers can explore the water tunnels, caves, and uninhabited islands *(see pp36–7)*.

# TOP10 ⭐ Phuket Town

The historical and administrative center of Phuket traces its roots back centuries – first to the early European traders and later to the Chinese immigrants who arrived here during the 19th-century tin-mining boom. Today, Phuket Town continues to thrive as one of the island's most authentic cultural areas, with magnificent architectural treasures, Chinese shrines, colorful markets, and restaurants that serve some of Phuket's most delicious local cuisines.

### Ko Sirey ①
Linked to Phuket Town via a small bridge, Sirey Island features hilly forest trails that wind their way through rubber plantations. Perched on a hilltop, Ko Sirey temple **(right)** enjoys sea views and features a large reclining Buddha image in its main hall.

### ② Sunday Walking Street Market
Thalang Road closes to traffic from 4pm every Sunday for this colorful market **(above)**, which offers many locally made craft items, along with clothes and good food stalls. The historic buildings here are illuminated for the occasion.

### ③ Naka Weekend Market
Located close to the Nakaram Temple on Virat Hongyok Road, this market is the ideal place for buying food, souvenirs and gifts, as well as a huge variety of clothing.

### ④ Marvelous Architecture
The distinctive style of architecture found in Phuket Town's old shop houses and mansions **(below)** is known as Sino-Portuguese. This highly attractive blend of Eastern and Western styles dates from the late 19th century (see pp14–15).

Phuket Town

Kutu

Phuket Town

⑦ ⑥ ⑨ ⑤ ② ① ③ ⑧ ⑩

### 7 Phuket Cultural Centre

Located on the Rajabhat University campus, this museum **(left)** houses old Thai shadow puppets, tin-mining artifacts, historic photographs, and books on local culture.

### 8 Suan Luang Park

This pleasant garden with lovely lotus ponds comes alive in the early mornings, when people come to exercise and perform Tai Chi.

#### ORIGINS OF THE VEGETARIAN FESTIVAL

In 1825, a traveling Chinese opera company in Kathu contracted malaria. According to legend, the afflicted nursed themselves back to health by following a strict vegetarian diet to purify their minds and bodies, and to honor the nine Emperor Gods of Chinese Taoism. After they recovered, the first Vegetarian Festival was held to thank the gods.

### 9 Rang Hill

Wonderful views of Phuket Town can be enjoyed from the summit of Rang Hill, where a breezy, tree-shaded park **(above)** also provides a relaxing venue for a picnic, some exercise, or simply reading a book.

### 10 Phuket Vegetarian Festival

This annual festival is held over nine days in late September/early October. Some devotees perform shocking rituals of self-mutilation, so it's not for the squeamish.

### 5 Chinese Shrines

Vibrant and colorful art can be admired at Chinese temples *(see pp46–7)* throughout the town. The shrines play an important role during the Chinese New Year and the annual Phuket Vegetarian Festival.

### 6 Monkey Hill

Although the views from atop nearby Rang Hill are more impressive, Monkey Hill offers a more unusual experience, as hordes of macaque monkeys congregate near the hilltop. Keep hold of your belongings – the monkeys may try to snatch them.

#### NEED TO KNOW
#### MAP K3

*Sunday Walking Street Market:* MAP P5; Thalang Road (between Phuket and Yaowarat roads); 4–10pm Sun

*Naka Weekend Market:* MAP J3; 4–10pm Sat & Sun

*Phuket Cultural Centre:* MAP K2; 21 Thepkasatri Road; 07621 1959 (ext 148); 8:30am–4:30pm Mon–Fri; closed weekends and public hols

■ Avoid walking tours at midday – the streets can be unbearably warm.

■ Try the iced coffee at Thungkha Kafae atop Rang Hill.

■ Sample a chili dog from the Tuk-Tuk Diner, which parks at the west end of the Thalang Road market.

# Historic Buildings in Phuket Town

**Blue Elephant Restaurant, set in elegant grounds**

### 1 Blue Elephant Restaurant

MAP N5 ■ 96 Krabi Road ■ 07635 4355 ■ Open 11am–10:30pm daily

Next door to the Chinpracha House, this former governor's mansion is a fine-dining venue and cookery school.

### 2 Standard Chartered Bank

MAP P5

This graceful Sino-Portuguese building once housed the country's oldest foreign bank. There are plans to convert it into a public museum.

### 3 Thai Hua Museum

MAP P5 ■ Thalang Road ■ 07621 1224 ■ Open 9am–5pm daily ■ Closed public holidays ■ Adm ■ thaihuamuseum.com

This distinctive building was once used as a schoolhouse. The museum provides an excellent overview of Phuket's tin-mining era. Displays cover the daily life of the Chinese immigrants, architecture, and archival photographs of old Phuket.

### 4 Chinpracha House

MAP N5 ■ 98 Krabi Road ■ 07621 1281 ■ Open 9am–4:30pm Mon–Sat, 9am–2:30pm Sun ■ Adm

This 19th-century mansion has served as a backdrop for several Hollywood films including Oliver Stone's 1993 movie *Heaven and Earth*, based on the Vietnam War. Now a museum of domestic life, the house stands as a timeless reminder of an earlier era.

### 5 House of the Beautiful Images

MAP P5 ■ Soi Romanee (Romani) 12 ■ 07621 4207 ■ Open 10am–9pm Thu–Tue ■ Closed Wed

Located on Soi Romanee (Romani), a charming street lined with wonderful buildings, the House of the Beautiful Images serves as a café specializing in breakfast and coffee. The space is also used to exhibit photography.

### 6 Dibuk Grill and Bar

MAP P5 ■ 69 Dibuk Road ■ 07625 8148 ■ Open 11am–11pm Mon–Sat

Another fine example of century-old architecture, this building now serves as a relaxing eatery known for its delicious Thai and French cuisine. The old Chinese-style house features soft interior lighting and antique fans.

**Facade of the Thai Hua Museum**

### 7 Phuket Philatelic Museum

MAP P5 ▪ Montri Road ▪ 07621 1020 ▪ Open 9:30am–5:30pm Tue–Sat

Also known as the Post Office Museum, this 20th-century building has displays detailing the history of the Thai postal service.

### 8 Phuket Provincial Hall

MAP Q4 ▪ Narisorn Road ▪ 07635 4875 ▪ Open 9am–5pm daily

The Provincial Hall was built in the early 1910s. It originally featured 99 doors and no windows, and is said to be the first reinforced concrete building in Thailand.

### 9 THAI Airways Office

MAP P5 ▪ 78 Ranong Road ▪ 07636 0444 ▪ Open 8am–5pm daily

The airline bought this mansion in 1947. The white, two-story building continues to serve as the THAI Airways Office in Phuket Town. It is believed to have been built in 1922.

### 10 China Inn Café and Restaurant

MAP P5 ▪ 20 Thalang Road ▪ 07635 6239 ▪ Open 11am–5pm Mon–Sat

Exquisite wooden doors, Chinese lanterns, and tiled floors decorate the entrance of this classic Sino-Portuguese-style house. The interior showcases a wonderful collection of old Chinese artifacts, while the highly regarded dining space is set in the backyard.

**Entrance to the China Inn Café**

## ARCHITECTURAL LEGACY

During the tin boom of the late 19th and early 20th centuries, countless Chinese immigrants arrived on Phuket seeking to capitalize on the island's new-found economic opportunities. The most successful tin barons built gorgeous colonial-style mansions. The architectural style, known as Sino-Portuguese, was derived from early European settlements. Examples abound in Phuket Town, particularly the shop houses and mansions on Dibuk, Thalang, Phang Nga, Rassada, Yaowarat, and Phuket roads.

**These Romanesque arched windows** are a typical element of the Sino-Portuguese architectural style.

**TOP 10**
**CHARACTERISTICS OF SINO-PORTUGUESE ARCHITECTURAL STYLE**

**1** Romanesque arched colonnades (porticoes)

**2** Inner courtyards (airwells)

**3** Exterior windows with Romanesque arches and shutters

**4** Double doors and double shutters

**5** Terracotta tiled roofs

**6** Tiled floors in ornate patterns

**7** Victorian ornamentation

**8** Chinese signage

**9** Ornamental wrought-iron gates

**10** Eaves decorated with ceramic shards

# TOP 10 ⭐ Wat Chalong

Historical records are unclear, but Wat Chalong was probably first built during the reign of King Rama II (r.1809–24). However, the temple has undergone many renovations since it was first erected. The complex features sacred imagery, including sculptures and murals of the Buddha's life. The holiest object is a bone fragment of the Buddha, now set in the Grand Pagoda. The temple is called Wat Chaitararam by royal decree, but everyone knows it as Wat Chalong.

**1 Architecture**
The temple's colorful, multitiered sloping roofs **(above)**, ornate exterior, and interior decorations are very picturesque. The Grand Pagoda's towering spire and glittering window frames are among its other visual highlights.

**2 Fortune Telling**
Fortune tellers sit inside the temple's main hall. They shake two cans of numbered bamboo sticks until one falls out. The number corresponds to a paper slip inside a wooden cabinet. Take it and ask for a translation.

**3 Merit-Making**
Thai Buddhists visit temples and pay respect to the Buddha, and other spiritual leaders, to accumulate merit, in the belief that such deeds will benefit one's position in this life and future lives **(left)**.

**4 Temple History**
During an uprising of Chinese tin workers in the late 19th century, many local Thais fled to Wat Chalong for protection. The temple's then abbot, Luang Pho Chaem, provided shelter to the people and was later honoured for this by King Rama V (r.1868–1910).

**5 Firecrackers**
Devotees burst firecrackers in thanks for answered prayers. The fireworks pop inside a beehive-shaped structure located outside, near the sermon hall.

### 6 Buddha Image

Known as Poh Than Jao Wat, the main Buddha image **(left)** is within Wat Chalong's western hall. It is flanked by two statues, one of which supposedly depicts a local man who won several lotteries after praying to the image.

### 7 Wax Figures

Lifelike models of former temple abbots can be found inside a special exhibition space. Visitors pay tribute to these spiritual leaders to make merit.

**WAT CHALONG FAIR**

First held in 1954, the annual Wat Chalong Fair transforms the temple grounds into a bustling entertainment venue featuring live music performances, sermons, and an endless variety of delicious local cuisine. Vendors also set up carnival games, ferris wheels, and merry-go-rounds. The eight-day festival coincides with the Chinese New Year and it historically marked the end of a local farm harvest.

**NEED TO KNOW**

**MAP J4** ■ Chao Fah Nok Road; 07621 1036, 07638 1893

**Open** 7am–5pm daily

■ Dress conservatively and remove your shoes before entering certain buildings. Don't turn your back on, or point your feet, at an image of the Buddha.

■ Street food vendors, selling everything from fried grasshoppers to grilled chicken and pork skewers marinated in chilli sauce, congregate outside the temple.

### 8 Wall Paintings

Inside the Grand Pagoda, wall paintings show events from the life of Siddhartha Gautama, who became the Buddha after gaining enlightenment. Notable depictions include him teaching his disciples and receiving offerings **(above)**.

### 9 Gilded Statues

Cast in bronze, these depictions of former temple abbots are covered in flecks of gold foil. Visitors offer donations and make merit by affixing small pieces of gold-colored foil onto the statues.

### 10 Grand Pagoda

This 197-ft (60-m) tall golden pagoda enshrines a bone splinter of the Buddha. Brought from Sri Lanka in 1999, it is housed inside a *chedi* (stupa) on the third story of the pagoda **(below)**.

# TOP 10 ⭐ Patong

Travelers dreaming of a sleepy tropical hideaway might want to look elsewhere – Patong is full of action. The most popular tourist area in Phuket, it features a great range of hotels, restaurants, and nightlife. Many of the high-end resorts are sheltered enclaves with lush gardens and private swimming pools. The seemingly endless shopping options, wild entertainment venues, and range of daytime activities make Patong the ultimate high-energy playground.

### 1 Patong Beach

Patong **(above)**, Phuket's most popular tourist beach, offers a range of attractions. It also has more laid-back areas – for peace and quiet, the northern end of the beach is best.

### 2 Massage and Spa Treatments

Thailand is known for its world-class hospitality, exemplified by its traditional massage treatments and spas, which are ubiquitous in Patong **(left)**.

### 3 Muay Thai Fights

Don't miss a chance to see this Thai martial art. Five three-minute rounds, accompanied by romping music, are preceded by the pomp and ceremony of ancient pre-fight rituals.

---

**NEED TO KNOW**

**MAP H3**

*Patong Boxing Stadium (Muay Thai fights):* **MAP P1**; 2/59 Sai Nam Yen Road; 07634 5185; adm B1,300 upward; www.boxingstadiumpatong.com

*Bangla Boxing Stadium (Muay Thai fights):* **MAP P2**;

Bangla Road; 07627 3222; adm B1,300 upward

*Banana Disco:* 124 Thaweewong Road; 07632 0306

*Seduction Discotheque:* 39/1 Bangla Road; 07634 0215; seduction disco.com

*Simon Cabaret:* Sirirach Road, Patong Beach;

07634 2011; www.phuket-simoncabaret.com

*Tiger Disco:* 49 Bangla Road; 07634 5112

- Be sure to barter with vendors at the market to get the best price.

- Street carts serve some of the best Thai food.

### ④ Water Sports

If you enjoy getting an adrenaline fix right at the beach, Patong is the place for you. From wave running and speedboat rides to parasailing and banana boats, Patong Bay offers a range of exhilarating marine activities **(left)**.

**A MATTER OF PERSPECTIVE**

Some foreign travelers are shocked by Patong's extremely liberal sexual norms, particularly after the sun goes down. The Bangla Road area is the nightlife epicenter of Patong, and it's not the place for families with young children. People-watching here can be an experience, but Bangla Road is not all Patong has to offer and it is easy to avoid if not to one's taste.

### ⑧ Street Markets

The night market sells everything from T-shirts to Buddha images, and prices are low. Those near the beach road offer the widest choice.

### ⑤ Fresh Seafood

At sundown, restaurants along the beachfront promenade display the day's fresh catch packed on ice. Snapper, grouper, shrimp, crabs, lobster, and other delicious seafood can be individually selected, grilled, and seasoned to your taste.

### ⑨ Bangla Road

The central vein of Patong is ablaze at night with neon lighting and has music blaring from every direction.

### ⑥ Discos

Patong's awesome nightlife needs little introduction. Some of the area's most popular party spots include Tiger Disco, Banana Disco, and Seduction Discotheque. Dance floors are packed, as DJs spin everything from garage to disco.

### ⑦ Cabaret Shows

These colorful shows, starring transvestites, have been thrilling audiences for decades. The most popular venue, Simon Cabaret **(left)**, puts on two shows in an extravagantly decorated theater.

### ⑩ Bars

As the island's bar capital, Patong boasts a huge range of places for enjoying a cold beer or cocktail, from traditional Irish pubs to open-air beer bars, and from go-go bars to sports pubs **(above)**.

# TOP 10 ⭐ Khao Phra Thaeo Royal Forest and Wildlife Reserve

Spread over 9 sq miles (23 sq km) of virgin rain forest, this national park in northeast Phuket provides one of the last remaining natural habitats for exotic and endangered animal species on the island. Visitors can immerse themselves in the jungles that once covered much of the island as Khao Phra Thaeo offers pristine forest, raw hiking trails, and picturesque waterfalls. There is also a rehabilitation center where gibbons receive care and treatment, as well as plenty of rare plants, flowers, and trees.

### 1 Gibbon Rehabilitation Project

The calls of gibbons ring through the forest around the center, which was established in 1992 to care for animals that had previously been living in captivity. It reintroduces some gibbons **(right)** into the wild.

### 2 Wildlife Conservation Development and Extension Centre

Located near the base of Ton Sai Waterfall, this visitor center offers lectures on the park's history and purpose, as well as trail guides, brochures, and limited, basic accommodations.

### 3 Bang Pae Waterfall

The larger of the park's two major waterfalls, Bang Pae **(left)** plummets down and forms a pool ideal for a cool, refreshing dip. The easy walk from the parking lot to the waterfall takes around ten minutes.

### 4 Ton Sai Waterfall

A scenic little waterfall in the center of the wildlife sanctuary, this is an enjoyable place to spend an afternoon. You can climb the rocky paths near the falls, but be careful, since the rocks can get slippery.

**NEED TO KNOW**
**MAP D5**

*Visitor Center:* 254 Moo 2, Thepkasattri Road, Thalang; 07631 1998; 8:30am–4:30pm daily; adm B200 (kids B100)

*Gibbon Rehabilitation Project:* Pa Khlock, Thalang; 07626 0492; 9am–4:30pm daily; www.gibbonproject.org

*Wildlife Conservation Development and Extension Centre:* Highway 4027; 07621 1067; 9am–4pm daily

*Zipline Tour:* Cable Jungle Adventure Phuket; 232/17 Bansuaneramit, Moo 8; 081977 4904; 9am–5pm daily; adm B2,150; www.cablejunglephuket.com

■ It can rain heavily without much warning, particularly during the summer months.

■ Try the Bang Rong Floating Restaurant near Bang Pae Waterfall.

### 8 Trekking
A scenic 5-mile- (8-km-) long jungle path links Ton Sai and Bang Pae waterfalls. At the visitor center near Ton Sai, trekkers can hire an experienced guide, who will be able to point out some of the park's exotic animal and plant species.

### 9 Virgin Rain Forest
Evergreen trees, bamboo forests, exotic orchids, ferns, and mosses can all be found in Khao Phra Thaeo, the last tract of virgin rain forest on the island. The area that surrounds the sanctuary includes several large rubber tree plantations.

### 10 Wildlife
The sanctuary's natural environment is home to a number of exotic species, including wild boar, macaque monkeys, gibbons, langurs, and various types of deer.

### 5 Zipline Tour
Sail with the birds and monkeys through the jungle canopy. Set just outside the forest reserve, the course is over a mile (2 km) long. Experienced guides take you through a full safety demonstration. It's a bit of a hike to the start of the course **(above)**.

### 6 Flora
An endangered plant known as the white-backed palm is one of the highlights of the Khao Phra Thaeo Royal Forest and Wildlife Reserve. Discovered by a German botanist in the 1950s, this elegant fan-shaped palm is unique to southern Thailand.

### 7 Bird-Watching
Northern Phuket is a true paradise for bird-watchers. Inside the sanctuary, you can spot flowerpeckers **(left)**, bulbuls, sunbirds, green Leafbirds, red-billed Malkohas, Asian fairy-bluebirds, blue-winged Pitta, and Brahminy Kites.

#### CAPTIVE GIBBONS
In many Thai tourist areas, local touts carry baby gibbons around to lure foreigners into taking photographs with the cute little primates. In exchange, the touts ask for a little money. If approached, keep in mind that the gibbons are being kept illegally, and that many of them lose their lives when hunters try to capture them for the tourist trade. The small Gibbon Rehabilitation Project at the Khao Phra Thaeo Royal Forest and Wildlife Reserve works to protect these animals.

# ★ Sirinat National Park

A rugged, pristine pine-lined strip runs along Phuket's northwest coast and marks three largely undeveloped beaches: Mai Khao, Nai Yang, and Nai Thon. Although this land forms the Sirinat National Park, over three quarters of the reserve's 35 sq miles (90 sq km) is marine territory. The clean waters feature large, healthy coral reefs, and Mai Khao Beach has become a well-known sea turtle nesting site. At the northern end of Sirinat is an unspoiled mangrove forest.

### 1 Upmarket Resorts

The beaches of northern Phuket are home to up-scale resorts that blend well with the national park surroundings. The JW Marriott **(below)**, Sala Phuket, and Anantara, among others, offer 5-star luxury *(see p112)*.

### 2 Camping on Nai Yang Beach

Visitors can bring their own tent to this beautiful beach, or rent one, priced at B225 per night, from the national park's Visitor Center. Different types of bedding and sleeping mats are also available. The well-kept campgrounds offer guests toilet and shower facilities.

### 3 Visitor Center

At the southern end of Mai Khao Beach, the Visitor Center has useful information, including maps. It rents out tents, plus budget bungalows at the north end of Nai Yang Beach.

**NEED TO KNOW**

*Visitor Center:* **MAP B3**; 89/1 Moo 1, Tambon Nai Yang; 07632 7152; 8:30am–4:30pm daily; park.dnp.go.th

*Mai Khao Marine Turtle Foundation:* **MAP B1**; 231 Moo3, Mai Khao, Talang, Phuket; 07633 8000 (ext 3309); www.maikhaomarineturtlefoundation.org

*Scuba Diving and Snorkeling:* **MAP B4**; Paradise Diving; 116 Moo 5, Sakoo Village, Thalang; 07632 8278; adm B3,290; www.dive-paradise.com

■ Those who cannot afford luxury resorts can pitch a tent on the beach.

■ Excellent fresh fish is served by the string of local seafood restaurants set along Route 402.

**Sirinat National Park**

### 9 Nai Thon Beach

This quiet beach **(left)** north of Bang Tao retains its sleepy and natural feel despite the coming of better road access. Small coral reefs located off either tip of the beach provide great opportunities for snorkeling.

### 5 Mangroves

A mangrove forest **(left)** can be found at the northern end of Mai Khao Beach. These unique trees, with their tangled roots visible above the shoreline, are crucial in maintaining the ecological balance.

### 6 Scuba Diving

Off the coast of northern Phuket lies an interesting scuba diving site – an old tin dredger that sank off the coast of Ko Waew. Reachable by boat from Nai Thon Beach, the 164-ft- (50-m-) long wreck rests at a depth of 53 ft (16 m).

### 7 Snorkeling

There are many opportunities for snorkeling near the rocky headlands of Nai Yang Beach. Masks, fins, and snorkels can be hired. Look out for colorful schools of fish.

### 8 Mai Khao Beach

Phuket's longest beach is a thin, undulating strip that slopes steeply down into the sea. Lined with magnificent screw pines, and with very little intrusive development, it remains one of the island's natural wonders **(below)**.

**TURTLE CONSERVATION**

The Mai Khao Marine Turtle Foundation, along with several Mai Khao Beach resorts, releases dozens of green turtles into the Andaman Sea each year to raise funds for the endangered sea turtles. The conservation effort also includes beach- and reef-cleaning projects. The number of turtles returning to Mai Khao Beach has dwindled, but it is hoped that the annual nesting site will be preserved.

### 10 Nature Trail

At the northern end of Mai Khao Beach, an elevated walkway loops through the mangrove forest, with signs pointing out exotic plant species, including black myrsina, Lady's Nails quisqualis, red cycas, and mountain ebony.

### 4 Sea Turtles

Giant sea turtles **(above)** return to Mai Khao Beach every year between November and March to lay their eggs. If you spot a turtle on the beach, do not disturb it or touch its eggs.

*Following pages* Floating bamboo-raft houses on Cheow Laan Lake, Khao Sok National Park

# TOP 10 ⭐ Naiharn Beach

Framing an idyllic bay on the island's southwestern tip, Naiharn Beach remains one of Phuket's most pristine waterfronts. The half-mile- (1-km-) long, white-sand beach is flanked by green hills and lapped by turquoise waters. While nearby Naiharn village has been modernized with cafés, art shops, and guesthouses, the beach and surrounding hills still maintain a tranquil, non-commercial vibe, with hotels congregated along only one end. During the high season, a number of private yachts drop anchor in the bay, making Naiharn their temporary home.

### 4 Naiharn Buddhist Monastery

Behind Naiharn Beach, this spiritual center **(below)**, which owns the beachfront, is said to be partly responsible for keeping it unspoiled. Visit at dawn, when locals make merit by offering food to the monks.

### 1 Naiharn Beach
Relax under a sun umbrella, catch a tan on the powdery white sand, or wade out into the emerald waters – Naiharn Beach **(above)** will satisfy even the toughest critic's ideal of a tropical paradise.

### 3 Surfing
The gently tumbling waves and sandy shoreline here attract many boogie-boarders; surfers go for the sandy beach break at the southern end or the reef break to the north. Beware of the undertow.

### 2 Yanui Beach
Just south of Naiharn Beach, and accessible via the road that leads to Phromthep Cape, this small V-shaped stretch of sand **(below)** offers seclusion amid the shade of coconut palms. It also has a small restaurant and a few simple bungalows.

**6 Naiharn Lake**
Bicyclists and joggers enjoy the paved half-mile (1-km) route encircling this inland freshwater lake. With sea breezes, it is also a pleasant picnic destination. Popular cafés and bars can be found on the lake's northwestern shore.

**5 Ao Sane Beach**
With its rocky shoreline and rough slope down into the sea, Ao Sane Beach (above) does not see hordes of swimmers. However, it is a prime spot for snorkelers, who claim that the visibility and nearby corals are among the best in Naiharn.

**7 Muay Thai**
A number of Muay Thai gyms have been established in Naiharn Village. Visitors can punch some heavy bags, skip rope, and hit the pads with former professional Thai fighters.

**EXPLOSIVE GROWTH**

Until the 21st century, the quiet beach and village at Naiharn were still unknown. The sleepy village had a few open-air restaurants and guesthouses, but not much more. Since 2010, like the rest of Phuket, development began, and residences, resorts, and restaurants started popping up throughout the town. Today, the beach is still one of Phuket's most beautiful, but attracts a lot more visitors than it did in the past.

**NEED TO KNOW**

**MAP H6**

*Sinbi Muay Thai:* **MAP H5**; 100/15 Moo 7, Sai Yuan Road, Rawai; 083 391 5535; www.sinbi-muaythai.com

*Rawai Supa Muay Thai:* **MAP H5**; 43/42 Moo 7, Soi Sai Yuan, Rawai; 07622 6495; www.supamuay thaiphuket.com

■ It is a long way from Naiharn village to the beach. Rent a car or motorbike to travel back and forth.

■ Drink fresh coconut water while at the beach.

**Phromthep Cape 8**
Crowds flock to the beach each evening to witness the vivid sunset over the Andaman Sea at sundown. Phromthep Cape (right) also has a market, restaurant, elephant shrine, and lighthouse.

**9 Beachside Lunch**
Shaded by a canopy of umbrellas and pine trees, the open-air restaurants at Naiharn Beach serve reasonably priced fresh fruit shakes, sandwiches, and a wide selection of Thai dishes.

**10 Windmill Viewpoint**
Perched high on the hills overlooking Naiharn Beach, the Phromthep Alternative Energy Station offers stunning views. Paragliders also launch from here to land on the beach.

# TOP 10 ⭐ Kata Beach

Located just south of Karon, the scenic Kata Beach, comprising two bays separated by a small rocky headland, offers an ideal balance of tropical scenery and well-developed tourism infrastructure. Kata has a number of high-end resorts, making it a popular destination for couples and families. Palm trees fringe the white-sand beach, and the clear turquoise waters offer good swimming conditions throughout the year. Visitors can even swim to nearby Ko Pu, a small island, passing beautiful coral reefs along the way.

### 1 Nightlife
Less wild than Patong, Kata still offers plenty for night owls. Most bars are open-air, dotted with festive lights, and play music aimed to please a crowd that wants to relax and chat (above).

### 2 Shopping
The beach vendors in Kata sell beachwear, coconuts, and snacks, while the off-beach stalls offer a wide range of inexpensive clothing and souvenirs.

### 3 Spa and Massage Treatments
Traditional Thai massage is available at numerous venues, including the canopy-covered massage beds along the beach.

### 4 Thai Cooking Classes
Learn how to make Thai curries and much more (below) at one of the many cookery classes in Kata. One is hosted by the upscale Boathouse restaurant, or there's the Kata Thai Cooking Class.

**NEED TO KNOW**

**MAP H5**

*Boathouse Wine and Grill:* Kata Beach; 07633 0015–7; adm (for cooking class) B2,600; www.boathousephuket.com

*Kata Thai Cooking Class:* 5 Ket Kwan Road, Kata Beach; 07628 4510; www.katathaicooking.com

*Kata Temple:* **MAP H4**; Patak Road, Karon; open daily

*Dino Park Mini-Golf:* **MAP H4**; Marina Phuket Resort, Karon Beach; 07633 0625; open 10am–11pm daily; adm B240 (kids B180); www.dinopark.com

■ Karon Viewpoint is a wonderful place to watch the sunset.

■ Wine lovers can visit the Boathouse Wine and Grill, whose excellent wine list features more than 800 labels.

### 7 Water Sports

The best season for surfing **(left)** in Kata is from May to October. The waters around Kata are great for beginners since the waves are not too large. The southern end is best for surfing, but if that's not for you, rent a kayak from the north end of the beach.

**DEVELOPMENT**

During the 1970s, Kata was known as a low-budget backpacker's destination offering inexpensive beach bungalows and cheap guesthouses. However, when Club Med opened its doors in 1985, the area started turning upscale. Today, Kata mostly caters to well-to-do family travelers. Low-cost rooms can still be found along the inland roads, while most of the beachfront properties have been snapped up by high-end developers.

### 9 Dino Park Mini-Golf

With a 39-ft- (12-m-) high waterfall and an erupting volcano, the setting at this miniature golf course is nothing short of stirring. Playing a round is a great way to beat the afternoon heat.

### 10 Kata Yai

When people talk about Kata, they are usually referring to Kata Yai **(below)**, which is the larger of the two Kata bays, and boasts more resorts and activities. The beach is separated from Kata Noi, which is much quieter, by a small rocky headland.

### 5 Karon Viewpoint

On the coastal road south toward Naiharn, this viewpoint provides gorgeous views of the island. Look north and you'll see three white-sand beaches along the coastline **(above)**.

### 8 Kata Noi

The more secluded of Kata's beaches, Kata Noi, located just south of Kata Yai, generally offers more space and privacy than its larger counterpart, especially during the low season.

### 6 Kata Temple

This Buddhist wat lies at the base of the mountains behind Kata town. Formally known as Wat Kittisangkaram, it dates from the 1800s, but it was rebuilt. It is rarely visited by tourists due to its modern buildings.

# TOP 10 ⭐ Similan Islands National Park

Soft white-sand beaches and emerald-colored waters are the foundations of this island paradise. Renowned as one of the world's top scuba diving destinations, the underwater world here is stunningly beautiful, with magnificent corals, colorful fish, and dramatic rock formations. The nine Similan islands also offer remarkable snorkeling. Plan your trip with a tour operator based on the mainland – diving equipment is not available on the islands.

### 1 Anita's Reef

This colorful reef **(below)** spreads across two Similan Islands, and is punctuated by large, dramatic boulders. Offering a relatively easy dive, Anita's Reef is often one of the first stops for live-aboard trips.

### 2 Ko Similan

Home to Donald Duck Bay **(above)**, named for the rock formation that resembles the cartoon character, Ko Similan is a perfect spot for you to pitch your tent. The island also has scenic walking trails, so carry sturdy shoes and a camera.

### 3 Live-Aboard Boats

One of the best ways to experience the dive sites around the Similans is to join a multiday trip on a live-aboard boat **(below)** offering guests several dives each day.

### 4 Christmas Point

Deep shelves, which are populated by white-tip reef sharks as well as ribbon eels, make this site very popular with divers and under-water photographers.

### NEED TO KNOW

*Visitor Center:* **MAP D2**; 93 Moo 5, Tambon Lam Kaen; 07645 3272; open 9am–5pm daily; adm B500 (kids B300; plus B200 per person for drivers); park.dnp.go.th

■ The park is closed May through October.

■ Food options are limited, so if you have special dietary needs, you should pack enough food to last your trip.

### 5 Beacon Reef

The longest reef in the Similan Islands, Beacon Reef also marks the place where the *Atlantis X* sank, with no casualties, in 2002. Today, the sunken vessel, now resting on a sloping coral wall, is one of the reef's most popular underwater attractions and provides home to a wide variety of marine life.

Ko Bangu

Ko Similan

Ko Payu

Ko Miang    Ko Ha

**Similan Islands National Park**

### 9 Richelieu Rock

Well known for its exotic marine life, Richelieu Rock has been renowned as a diving site since whale sharks and manta rays were spotted here.

**DIVING PRECAUTIONS**

Scuba diving is very safe when done correctly, but it can be dangerous – even deadly – for the untrained diver. Reliable dive companies require all participants to have a PADI (Professional Association of Diving Instructors) certification. A number of companies on Phuket are licensed to provide courses and certification. The PADI course for beginners is called "Open Water Diver" and can be completed in a few days. Visit www.padi.com for a list of PADI dive centers in Thailand.

### 7 Ko Bon

Located in a protected bay and featuring one of Thailand's only vertical dive walls, this site, off Ko Bon, provides marvelous opportunities to see leopard sharks and manta rays **(left)**.

### 10 East of Eden

A brilliantly colorful reef, East of Eden is one of the most popular dive sites in the Similan Islands. Teeming with fish, it offers a wide diversity of marine life – coral, sea fans, and more.

### 6 Elephant Head Rock

The largest pinnacle in the Similan Islands juts above the water in a peculiar shape that lends this dive site its name. With its underwater caverns, tunnels, and swim-throughs, this site is home to numerous fish, including small, black-tip reef sharks.

### 8 Ko Miang

Home to the national park headquarters, Ko Miang **(right)** is the second biggest island in the Similans. Visitors will find campsites and basic bungalows (some with air-conditioned rooms). A large tent can be rented here for around B450 a night.

# ⭐ Khao Sok National Park

With a landmass of more than 270 sq miles (700 sq km), this park, about 110 miles (177 km) north of Phuket, is southern Thailand's largest virgin forest. Older and more diverse than even the Amazon rain forest, Khao Sok is home to numerous exotic animal and plant species, and has breathtaking natural scenery. Nature lovers will find inspiration in the park's majestic limestone cliffs, its rough jungle trails, and its beautiful, placid waterways.

### 1 Canoeing and Kayaking

The scenic Sok river offers a relaxing way to experience the park's natural wonders. Kayak or canoe through lush jungle, past towering limestone rocks. You may spot snakes, exotic hornbills, and long-tail macaque monkeys.

### 3 Cheow Laan Lake

Surrounded by verdant forests and towering mountains, this beautiful lake (above) was formed when Ratchaprapha Dam was constructed in 1982. It makes for a perfect retreat for those looking for a quiet day.

### 4 Raft Houses

Thatched-roof floating raft houses line the banks of Cheow Laan Lake (below), and visitors may stay in them for a night or longer. When the sun rises in the morning, dive into the lake for a brisk morning swim or enjoy a canoe ride.

### 2 Waterfalls

There are several scenic waterfalls (above) in the park, although finding them sometimes requires the assistance of a local guide. Bang Hua Raet, Wang Yao, and Wing Hin waterfalls are all located within a 1-mile (2-km) radius of the park headquarters.

**6 Wildlife**
A bird-watcher's paradise, Khao Sok National Park has numerous exotic bird and mammal species including hornbills, kingfishers **(left)**, wild pigs, eagles and much more. Wildlife enthusiasts may even spot Asiatic black bears (see pp34–5).

**BUA PHUT**

These huge red flowers, whose diameter can reach up to 35 inches (90 cm), are popular with visitors, although finding one in bloom often requires good timing and the help of a local guide. Known scientifically as *Rafflesia kerrii*, the flowers are abundant from January to March, and have a pungent odor to attract flies for pollination. The species is endangered.

**7 Night Safaris**
As some animal species, such as the loris and the leopard cat, can only be spotted after dark, night river safaris are a popular way to see these unique creatures. Canoes or bamboo rafts are used to quietly glide down the Sok river.

**8 Bamboo Rafting**
Float down the Sok on a unique watercraft fashioned out of lengths of bamboo, taking in the trees, magnificent mountains, and wildlife. You'll stop for lunch in a riverside restaurant.

**10 Caves**
Experience the tantalizing darkness of some of the park's many caves, including the popular Tham Nam Talu and Ha Roi Rai. These grottoes have fascinating stalagmites and stalactites **(below)**, as well as legions of bats.

**9 Jungle Trekking**
Walk along well-beaten paths with a guide through the untamed, lush jungle. The scope for trekking is exceptional, with caves, waterfalls, and lakes.

Cheow Laan Lake

Park HQ

Sok

401

**Khao Sok National Park**

**5 Romanee Hot Spring**
Located just south of the National Park, this natural hot spring has been attractively developed with tiled pools, and the mineral waters are excellent for relieving muscle stress from strenuous trekking activities.

**NEED TO KNOW**

*Visitor Center:* **MAP F1**; Moo 6, Khlong Sok; 07739 5139; 8am–4pm daily; adm B300 (kids B150); park.dnp.go.th

*Raft Houses, Bamboo Rafting, Jungle Trekking:* **MAP F1**; Elephant Hills Tented Camp; 170 Moo 7, Tambon Khlong Sok; 07638 1703; www.elephanthills.com

*Canoeing and Kayaking, Adventure Trips:* **MAP F1**; Paddle Asia; 18/58 Radanusorn; 07624 1519; www.paddleasia.com

■ Khao Sok can be visited on a day trip from Phuket, but it is better appreciated with more time.

■ Romanee Hot Spring visits are organized via Hotel Khao Sok (www.hotelkhaosok.com/tours).

# Exotic Animal Species in Khao Sok National Park

**Malaysian tapir on the move**

### 1 Malaysian Tapir

With its distinctive proboscis, this large-bodied herbivore looks somewhat like a pig with an elephant's trunk. The tapir's black color provides camouflage, so that, when it is lying down, the animal looks like a rock.

### 2 Bamboo Rat

Sporting short bulky bodies covered in spiky fur, these nocturnal rodents live predominantly in bamboo thickets, as well as in grasslands and forests. Bamboo rats have sharp teeth and claws that are ideally suited to digging the burrows in which they sleep during the day.

### 3 Barking Deer

Also known as muntjac, these small, brown-haired deer have short antlers. Commonly seen in the park, they are called barking deer because they are known to bark when they sense danger.

**Barking deer**

### 4 Tiger

Many of Thailand's 200 to 250 remaining wild tigers are believed to be living in Khao Sok, although you are unlikely to catch a glimpse of one. If you are lucky, however, you might come across tiger tracks.

### 5 Cobras

Khao Sok is home to four different species of cobra – the monocled, spitting, king, and Asian cobras. The king cobra is the world's longest venomous snake, reaching lengths greater than 16 ft (5 m).

**Striking hornbill, perched in a tree**

### 6 Hornbill

The hornbill's distinctive yellow/red horn and long down-curved mandible make the bird easily identifiable. Feeding on fruits, berries, insects, small mammals, and eggs, hornbills often reside in dense forests. Many species can be spotted in Khao Sok National Park.

### 7 Tarantula

These massive spiders tend to dwell inside underground burrows. The ones found in Thailand move fast and are known to be aggressive, so give the tarantula plenty of space if you encounter one in the wild.

### (8) Clouded Leopard

Exceptional climbers, with large feet and powerful claws, clouded leopards have a beautiful yellow-brown coat with distinctive cloud markings. The animal sleeps in trees and can hang upside down from branches by its hind paws. Its prey includes small mammals and birds, among other creatures.

### (9) Elephant

Wild elephants still roam Khao Sok National Park but sadly, these majestic creatures, the symbol of Thailand, are an endangered species. Herds of elephants can occasionally be spotted in forested areas near watering holes and elsewhere.

### (10) Malaysian Sun Bear

A small bear that generally weighs less than 143 lb (65 kgs), this threatened animal resides in dense forests, where it sleeps and suns itself in trees. An omnivore, the sun bear has no real predators, other than the occasional human.

**Malaysian Sun Bear foraging**

## HISTORY OF THE PARK

Before it was declared a national park in 1980, the forest-covered land known as Khao Sok was a wilderness that stretched to Myanmar. Few roads bisected this territory, and animal populations, including tigers, flourished. When Ratchaprapha Dam was built in the mid-1980s, numerous trees were chopped down. Poachers also threatened the stability of some animal populations. Today, under the protection of the National Park Service, Khao Sok is home to lots of exotic species, and many poachers have become conservationists.

**Liana vines** string themselves from tree to tree, forming sky bridges used by wildlife to get about.

**TOP 10
FLORA IN KHAO SOK
NATIONAL PARK**

1 Rain forest vegetation
2 Coconut palms
3 Buttressed roots trees
4 Ficus trees
5 Bamboo trees
6 Tropical pitcher plants
7 Dipterocarps trees
8 *Rafflesia kerrii*
9 Banana trees
10 Liana vines

# TOP 10 ⭐ Phang Nga Bay

Just east of Phuket over 40 small islands dot the brilliantly azure waters of Phang Nga Bay. Wind and water have eroded these limestone karst islets into a variety of extraordinary shapes that tower above the water's surface. This National Park is home to an abundance of flora and fauna that thrive amidst the crevices, arches, tide pools, caves, and coastal forests. Paddling a sea kayak amongst the grandeur of these soaring peaks is an experience to savor, but motorized boats can also transport you around the bay.

### 3 James Bond Island

The backdrop for 007's infamous duel in *The Man with the Golden Gun*, the island – also known as Ko Khao Phing Kan – today represents one of Phuket's most popular island day trips **(right)**.

### 4 Diving

Several popular dive sites, including the sunken passenger ferry, *King Cruiser*, can be found in Phang Nga Bay. You can also snorkel to coral reefs.

### 1 Kayaking

Paddle through extraordinary aquatic grottoes that open into magnificent open-air lagoons **(above)**, populated by exotic birds such as hornbills and kingfishers. The pristine jungle scenery beside these lagoons is also worth exploring on foot.

### 5 Ko Phanak

This island is favored by sea kayakers because of its abundance of hongs – amazing hidden sea chambers that are open to the sky but enclosed by the island, and accessible only though caves.

### 6 Khao Khian

Also known as "Writing Hill," this cave has ancient drawings of humans, birds, fish, and other marine life, dating back some 3,000 years.

### Ko Panyee 2

Most of Ko Panyee's landmass is consumed by a towering limestone rock. Due to this geology, it is difficult to build on the island, and the village has been constructed on stilts above the shallow waters of the south coast **(right)**.

### (7) Chinese Junk Boat Cruises

One of Phuket's classic boat cruises, the Chinese junk-rigged schooner *June Bahtra* explores the legendary islands and limestone cliffs of Phang Nga Bay, while a separate evening cruise trip provides sundown dinner and cocktails.

### (9) National Park Headquarters

The park headquarters, near Phang Nga town, features a raised walkway through a mangrove wetland, as well as boat rentals, a restaurant, and good bungalows. Phang Nga town pier is also a staging point for boats to the islands.

**Phang Nga Bay**

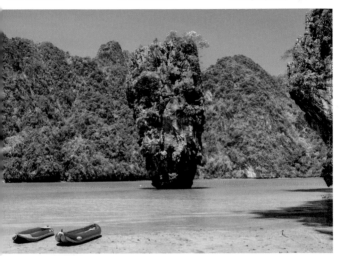

### (10) Mangrove Wetlands

Phang Nga Bay has the largest mangrove forests in Thailand, with the best on the mainland at the north end of the bay. Kayaks let you get up close to their twisted underwater root systems **(left)**.

### (8) Ko Yao Noi

With unspoiled coastlines, pristine beaches, and pretty thatched-roof bungalows, this island – part of a two-island group – exudes tranquil vibes.

**NEED TO KNOW**

*Visitor Center:* **MAP F2**; 80 Moo 1, Tambon Ban Tha Dan, Ko Panyee; 07648 1188; 8am–4pm daily; adm B300 (kids B100); park.dnp.go.th

*Diving:* **MAP H4**; Sunrise Divers; 269/24 Patak Road, Karon Plaza, Karon Beach; www.sunrise-divers.com

*Chinese Junk Boat Cruises:* **MAP F2**; Asian Oasis; 8am–6pm daily; & 4–9pm daily;

adm B3,700 onward (day), B2,500 onward (evening); www.asian-oasis.com

*Kayaking:* **MAP F2**; John Gray's Sea Canoe; adm B3,950 onwards; www. johngray-seacanoe.com

■ Hire a long-tail boat at Naiharn Beach to visit some of the islands.

■ Support locals – buy food and refreshments if they're selling them.

# The Top 10
# of Everything

**Murals at Wat Chalong depicting
scenes from the Buddha's life**

# Top 10 Moments in History

**Mural depicting the attempted Burmese invasion of 1785**

### 1 1st Century BC– AD 2nd Century: Earliest Records

Phuket was founded by Indian merchants, with trade dating back to the 1st century BC. It was later mentioned by the Greek geographer Ptolemy, who referred to it as "Junk Ceylon," a "cape" en route to the Malaysian peninsula.

### 2 AD 1500–1700: Tin Seekers

Tin defined Phuket's economy for hundreds of years. The Dutch established a strategic trading presence in Phuket after it was discovered that the island had vast tin reserves. The English and French followed shortly after, and the Siamese King Narai (r.1656–88) granted France monopoly in 1685.

### 3 AD 1688: French Expulsion

After the Siamese revolution of 1688, in which the pro-foreign Siamese King Narai was overthrown, the French were ordered out of Siam. The French, under General Marshal Desfarges, captured Phuket in an attempt to reassert influence in Siam in 1689, but the occupation of the island was futile.

### 4 March 13, 1785: Burmese Invasion Repelled

Led by two sisters – Thao Thep Kasattri and Thao Srisoonthorn – the Siamese defended Phuket against a month-long Burmese attack. Francis Light, an English ship captain, had alerted Phuket of assembling Burmese forces, giving the army time to prepare.

### 5 Early 19th Century: Chinese Immigration

Lured by Phuket's flourishing tin mines, and to escape poverty in their own country, thousands of Chinese workers immigrated to the island during the early 1800s, establishing communities and customs that define Phuket to the present day. Chinese shrines, architecture, and festivals are among their legacies.

### 6 1876: Tin Worker Rampage

A group of migrant Chinese tin workers, disgruntled over their low wages and difficult living conditions, instigated a violent uprising on Phuket, causing local residents to flee to Wat Chalong for protection. The monks of the temple sheltered the people and eventually helped restore calm to the island.

**7 1933: Phuket Province**

During the reign of King Rama V (r.1868–1910), Phuket solidified its role as the administrative center of the southern provinces. The island was, however, only a rural subdivision at the time. It became a full province in 1933.

**8 1970s: Phuket "Discovered"**

Although the island had been a hotbed of international economic activity for centuries, some still claim that Phuket was "discovered" by Western backpackers in the 1970s. It is true, however, that the revival in travel during this decade led to the creation of tourism infrastructure.

**9 26 December 2004: Indian Ocean Tsunami**

The devastation caused by the tsunami was immense – thousands of lives lost in a matter of minutes. In Thailand, the tsunami represented the worst natural disaster in history, leaving some 8,000 people dead. Busy merchant streets became lethal rapids, and everything on Ko Phi Phi was essentially washed away.

Aftermath of the 2004 tsunami

**10 May 2014: Military Coup**

After Prime Minister Yingluck Shinawatra was ousted for involvement in a corrupt rice-buying scheme, the new military leaders began a nationwide anti-corruption campaign. Phuket was an early target: officials working with illegal developers, the taxi mafia, and pushy beach vendors were all called to account.

**TOP 10 HISTORICAL FIGURES**

**Portrait of King Rama V**

**1 René Charbonneau (17th century)**
This French medical missionary once served as the governor of Phuket.

**2 Alexandre Chevalier de Chaumont (1640–1710)**
France's first ambassador to Siam was granted the country's tin monopoly in 1685.

**3 Thao Thep Kasattri (18th century)**
This gutsy Thai woman and her sister rallied Siamese troops to rise up against the Burmese invasion.

**4 Thao Srisoonthorn (18th century)**
The Heroines' Monument was built in honor of Thao Srisoonthorn and her sister Thao Thep Kasattri.

**5 Captain Francis Light (1740–94)**
This British colonial officer alerted the administration in 1785 that Burmese troops were massing for an attack.

**6 King Rama V (1853–1910)**
Rama V was credited with modernizing Siam and preventing the nation from being colonized by Western powers.

**7 Luang Pho Chaem (19th century)**
The abbot of Wat Chalong, this monk sheltered local residents during a violent tin worker uprising in 1876.

**8 Khaw Sim Bee (1857–1913)**
A Chinese immigrant who started the Thai rubber industry, Khaw was made governor of Phuket by Rama V.

**9 Mom Luang Tridosyuth Devakul (20th century)**
Hotelier and restaurateur, Mom Tri has helped raise Phuket's luxury standards since the 1980s.

**10 Pote Sarasin (1905–2000)**
The Sarasin Bridge (completed 1967) was named after this Thai politician.

# 🔟 Museums and Monuments

**Kathu Mining Museum, housed in a grand mansion**

### ① Kathu Mining Museum
MAP J2 ■ Kathu-Ko Kaeo Road, Kathu district ■ Open 8am–4pm Mon–Sat ■ Adm

Paying tribute to Phuket's rich tin-mining heritage, this museum has dioramas of early mining techniques, caves, and workers in action. Other exhibits in the Sino-Portuguese style mansion show tin-dredging operations and a model of an opium den.

### ② Phuket Seashell Museum
MAP H5 ■ 12/2 Moo 2, Viset Road, Rawai ■ 07661 3666 ■ Open 8am–6pm daily ■ Adm ■ www.phuket seashell.com

Housing a private collection, the Phuket Seashell Museum has more than 2,000 varieties of seashells, including one weighing 550 lb (250 kg), as well as the world's largest golden pearl.

### ③ Thai Hua Museum

Originally built to serve as a Thai-Chinese school, this 100-year-old structure *(see p14)* today functions as a museum, exhibition space, and function hall.

Visitors can stroll through the old schoolhouse, which has interesting displays depicting daily life during this period.

### ④ Thalang National Museum

Phuket's national museum *(see p92)* has a range of displays on the Battle of Thalang, tin mining, sea gypsies, and the history of the Chinese on Phuket. A magnificent 9th-century Vishnu statue, discovered in the 20th century, stands in the main hall.

### ⑤ Saphan Hin Mining Monument
MAP K3 ■ Near Phuket Town, Phuket Road

Located in a waterfront park, this monument is dedicated to Edward Miles, the Australian ship captain who brought the first tin dredgers to Phuket in 1909.

### ⑥ Big Buddha

This 148-ft- (45-m-) tall Buddha *(see p82)* sits high atop Nakkerd Hill, with sweeping 360-degree views that stretch from Chalong Bay to the

**Burmese marble Big Buddha**

Andaman Sea. Carved from white Burmese marble, the Buddha sits cross-legged on a podium decorated with lotus flowers. This is a peaceful, spiritual site.

## 7 Phuket Philatelic Museum

**MAP P5 ■ Montri Road, Phuket Town ■ 07621 1020 ■ Open 8:30am–4:30pm Mon–Fri, 9am–noon Sat**

Dedicated to Thailand's post office, this philately museum is housed in an 80-year-old building in Phuket Town. Old telephones, scales, tele-type machines, and stamps can be seen here, along with displays on the history of the Thai post office since its beginnings under King Rama V.

## 8 Phuket Cultural Centre

This center has a collection of old artifacts that helps tell the cultural history of Phuket and southern Thailand. Visitors might want to request a guide, since most of the information is in Thai (see p13).

**Embroidery, Phuket Cultural Centre**

## 9 Thavorn Hotel Lobby Museum

**MAP P5 ■ 74 Rassada Road, Phuket Town ■ 07621 1333–5**

In this magnificent wood-paneled hotel lobby, visitors will discover a fascinating collection of vintage photographs of old Phuket Town and Thai royalty, memorabilia such as classic Thai movie posters, movie projectors, opium pipes, tin-mining equipment, and a range of traditional Chinese wedding hats.

**Marigolds on Heroines' Monument**

## 10 Heroines' Monument

**MAP C6 ■ Thepkasatri Road, north of Phuket Town**

Unveiled in 1967, this monument depicts the two sisters who stalled a Burmese invasion in 1785 by leading women dressed in army uniforms out into the field (see p40). The Burmese forces thought that these troops were reinforcements from Bangkok, and withdrew.

# 🔟 Buddhist Temples

**Temple building at Wat Chalong**

### 1 Wat Chalong
Phuket's most visited temple comprises a number of ornately decorated buildings, which were built at different times. The temple holds statues of former monks and lifelike wax models. Sometimes, there are firecracker displays of gratitude for answered prayers from devotees. The annual Wat Chalong Fair is held at the temple around Chinese New Year *(see pp16–17)*.

### 2 Wat Prathong
Built in the 1750s, and known locally as Wat Phra Phut, this temple *(see p91)* is Phuket's second most important after Wat Chalong. The half-buried golden Buddha statue is the main attraction. According to legend, anyone who tries to uproot the statue will be cursed.

### 3 Wat Suwan Khiri Khet
MAP H4 ■ Patak Road, Karon
■ Open 8am–5:30pm daily
Also known as Wat Karon because of its location, this temple features engravings depicting scenes from the Buddha's life on the doors and windows. Two fantastic turquoise *naga* serpents encircle the main temple building and form railings down to the entrance. A smaller building guarded by a statue of a yak (mythical character in the Thai *Ramayana*) houses an attractive black sapphire Buddha image.

### 4 Wat Kathu
MAP J2 ■ Moo 4 Baankathu, Kathu ■ Open 8am–5:30pm daily
Located just outside Patong, this temple offers a peaceful respite from the surrounding frenzy of tourist activity. Its red windows are decorated in gilt-covered reliefs depicting scenes from the Buddha's life; colored glass and tiles decorate the exterior.

### 5 Wat Suwan Kuha
MAP F2 ■ Phang Nga
■ Open 8am–5:30pm daily ■ Adm
This temple is popularly known as Monkey Temple, for the throngs of pesky animals that reside within its grounds and beg for, or steal, food. The actual Buddhist monuments here are located inside a breathtaking cave, with a massive reclining Buddha image forming the centerpiece. Located in Phang Nga, this Buddhist temple is a popular stop for day-trippers from Phuket.

**Reclining Buddha of Wat Suwan Kuha**

### 6 Wat Kosit Wihan
MAP K2 ■ Highway 402
■ Open 8am–5:30pm daily

It's a bit of a climb to this temple carved into a hillside, but the reward is great views of Phuket Town. In the grounds stands a large Buddhist cemetery, and a number of small monuments with photographs of the people who were cremated here.

### 7 Wat Phranang Sang
MAP C5 ■ Thepkasattri Road
■ Open 8am–5:30pm daily

Built over 200 years ago, Phuket's oldest temple houses the mummi-fied relics of a former abbot, Luang Poh Bai, and a collection of large tin Buddha images, crafted when tin was still considered a semiprecious metal. The Heroines' Monument (see p43) stands near this temple.

**Temple interior, Wat Phranang Sang**

### 8 Wat Srisoonthorn
MAP C6 ■ Thepkasattri Road
■ Open 7am–5:30pm daily

Towering above this temple is a massive 95-ft- (29-m-) tall reclining Buddha statue, depicting the Buddha as he achieved Enlightenment. Nine other Buddha statues populate the entranceway. Built in 1792, and known locally as Wat Lipon, the temple was later renamed Wat

Srisoonthorn to commemorate one of the two sisters (see p41) who defended Phuket from foreign conquerors in the 18th century.

### 9 Wat Putta Mongkol
MAP P5 ■ Dibuk Road, Phuket Town ■ Open 8am–5:30pm daily

Located in the heart of Phuket Town, this temple is sometimes referred to as Wat Klang (literally, central temple). It features colorful archi-tectural designs, including yellow *chedis* (stupas), as well as an old Sino-Portuguese colonial home, which is used as the monks' dormitory. The spacious grounds are also home to the Phuket Buddhist Association and Phuket Old Town Foundation.

### 10 Wat Kajonrangsan
MAP N5 ■ Ranong Road, Phuket Town ■ Open 7am–5:30pm daily

A unique temple in Phuket Town, Wat Kajonrangsan, also called Wat Kajon, features distinctive Roman-style architecture in the *ubosot* (ordination chapel). Since it does not draw busloads of tourists, a visit here offers a good opportunity to observe an active community environment. The temple grounds also house a school.

# **TOP10 Chinese Shrines**

**Colorful dragon motifs on the Tha Rua Chinese Shrine**

### **1 Tha Rua Chinese Shrine**
MAP J1 ■ Thepkasattri Road
■ Open 6am–6pm daily

Tha Rua, the largest Chinese temple in Phuket, has undergone a series of massive renovations, reported to cost upwards of B40 million and funded entirely by private donations. Colorful, with bold dragon motifs and brightly lit at night, the new Tha Rua Chinese Shrine is far more elaborate in scale than its predecessor.

### **2 Put Jaw Chinese Temple**
MAP N5 ■ Soi Phuthorn, Ranong Road, Phuket Town ■ Open 6:30am–8pm daily ■ Adm

The island's oldest Chinese temple is dedicated to the goddess of mercy.

Those suffering from ill-health often come here to pray for relief, and the monks can prescribe Chinese herbal medicines. The temple helps parents name their newborn babies.

### **3 Kathu Shrine**
MAP J2 ■ Kathu Village
■ Open 8am–5:30pm daily

Credited as the first Chinese shrine on Phuket to celebrate the annual Vegetarian Festival *(see p13)*, this temple features a fascinating collection of intricately designed Taoist deity statues that are the main objects of worship at the shrine.

### **4 Boon Kaw Kong Shrine**
MAP H2 ■ Patong Road
■ Open 9am–5pm daily

Drivers often honk their car horns for good luck as they pass by this revered shrine located on the hilltop between Patong and Kathu. Besides simply hoping for good fortune, the drivers are also acknowledging the ghosts of travelers who have died while passing over the hill in the past. Well integrated in the local community, this small but popular shrine frequently shows films on a giant outdoor screen.

**Worshipers, Put Jaw Chinese Temple**

### ⑤ Bang Niew Shrine

MAP Q6 ■ Ong Sim Phai Road, Phuket Town ■ Open 7am–5:30pm daily

Built in 1934 and destroyed twice by fire, this shrine – also known as Tao Bong Keng or Chai Tueng – plays a key role in the Vegetarian Festival. Here, one may see devotees with bizarre piercings, or walking across red-hot coals. The shrine houses deities believed to assist worshipers with their career aspirations.

### ⑥ Sam San Shrine

MAP N5 ■ Krabi Road, Phuket Town ■ Open 8am–5:30pm daily

Built in 1853 and dedicated to Mazu, the Chinese goddess of the sea, this shrine frequently hosts ceremonies to consecrate new boats before their maiden sea voyage. The shrine pays homage to the patron saint of sailors, and also features a number of intricate carvings.

### ⑦ Shrine of the Serene Light

MAP P5 ■ Chao Fah Nok Road ■ 07621 1036, 07621 2213 ■ Open daily

Built by a local Chinese family more than 100 years ago, this historic shrine, once hidden down a narrow alleyway, can be viewed directly from Thalang Road today. Brightly colored ornamentation adorns the roof of the shrine's red-pillared entranceway.

### ⑧ Cherngtalay Shrine

MAP B6 ■ Thalang District ■ Open 7am–5:30pm daily

Popular with local community members who seek healing from the shrine's deities, Cherngtalay Shrine dates back more than 100 years to the founding of a settlement of Chinese tin-mine workers. The ornately decorated tile roof depicts eight immortal Chinese gods, along with the colorful dragon imagery common to many of these temples.

**Entrance to Jui Tui Chinese Temple**

### ⑨ Jui Tui Chinese Temple

MAP N5 ■ Soi Phuthorn, Ranong Road, Phuket Town ■ Open 8am–5:30pm daily

This colorful Taoist temple, dedicated to the vegetarian deity Kiu Wong In, plays a central role in the Vegetarian Festival. Originally built in 1911 on Soi Romanee, the first Jui Tui temple was destroyed by a fire and rebuilt at its current location.

### ⑩ Kuan Te Kun Shrine

MAP K1 ■ Sapam Village ■ Open 8am–5:30pm daily

Though less prominent, and on a smaller scale, than some of the other shrines on Phuket, Kuan Te Kun – commonly known as Sapam Shrine – is still worth visiting due to its picturesque appearance. With brilliantly colored dragons encircling its four main pillars and guarding its entrance, Kuan Te Kun is full of photo opportunities.

# 🔟 Picturesque Places

### 1 Ko Phi Phi Leh

With dramatic limestone cliffs giving way to white sand and blue lagoons, this uninhabited island is a tropical paradise. Day-trippers enjoy snorkeling and swimming in the placid Andaman waters, as well as seeing the 400-year-old wall paintings by fishermen in the Viking Cave. You can also visit Maya Bay, where *The Beach* was filmed *(see p100)*.

**Donald Duck Bay on Ko Similan**

### 2 Similan Islands

One of the top scuba diving destinations in the world, the Similan Islands *(see pp30–31)* are home to rare marine life, including magnificent coral reefs, as well as pristine, unpopulated beaches. Accommodation on overnight snorkeling or diving trips is in tents or very basic bungalows on the beach.

### 3 Phang Nga Bay

Verdant limestone cliffs jut up from this bay, with James Bond Island one of the most popular of these land masses. To escape the crowds, look for full-day sea canoe journeys through aquatic grottoes and tunnels *(see pp36–7)*.

### 4 Rang Hill

With sweeping views of Phuket Town and wide expanses of green ideal for picnics, the top of Rang Hill is one of Phuket's most relaxing spots. People come here to exercise or read a book. Others enjoy the restaurants with magnificent views and the island's best iced coffee. The bronze statue of a former governor stands near the viewpoint *(see p13)*.

### 5 Khao Sok National Park

Beautiful lakes, thrilling caves, and limestone cliffs are interspersed with ancient evergreen trees in this virgin forest north of Phuket. Home to a diverse population of wildlife, as well as rare tree species, Khao Sok offers some of the best trekking, canoeing, and safaris in southern Thailand *(see pp32–5)*.

### 6 Phromthep Cape

Dramatic, swirling shades of red, purple, and orange appear on the horizon during the sunset crescendo at Phromthep Cape *(see p27)*. The hilltop viewpoint also has restaurants, an outdoor market, an elephant shrine, and a lighthouse.

### 7 Mangroves

These trees, with their tangled and exposed roots, can be found along Phuket's muddy shorelines. Sea canoe tours offer the best way to see the mangroves up close. They are home to crab-eating macaque monkeys, while underwater they serve as nurseries for crustaceans and fish. The trees themselves are picturesque – and unusual, because they survive in saltwater.

**Sailing Phang Nga Bay**

### ⑧ Sirinat National Park

Located in northwest Phuket, Sirinat National Park *(see pp22–3)* protects some of Phuket's last mangroves, as well as pristine beaches including Mai Khao Beach, a nesting sites for sea turtles. An elevated nature trail guides visitors through the mangrove forests, with signs explaining the various species.

### ⑨ Cheow Laan Lake

Surrounded by tree-covered limestone cliffs, this stunning lake in the heart of Khao Sok National Park is scattered with floating bamboo-raft houses. In the early morning, the lake's long-tail boats and mist-shrouded shores provide excellent material for photographers. Monkeys, wild boars, and gibbons populate the surrounding forest *(see p32)*.

**Floating homes on Cheow Laan Lake**

### ⑩ Bang Pae Waterfall

At a height of 59 ft (18 m), this isn't exactly a breathtaking plummet of water, but Bang Pae Waterfall offers a picturesque backdrop for swimming. Located close to the Gibbon Rehabilitation Project in the Khao Phra Thaeo Royal Forest and Wildlife Reserve, it is best visited during the rainy season between June and November *(see p20)*.

---

**BEST PHUKET VIEWPOINTS**

**View from Big Buddha**

**1 Karon Viewpoint**
This has breathtaking views of Kata Noi, Kata, and Karon beaches, plus a sheltered viewing pavilion *(see p29)*.

**2 Laem Singh Viewpoint**
**MAP G1**
Above the beach of the same name, there is a covered platform with seating.

**3 Windmill Viewpoint**
**MAP H6**
A good alternative to the sometimes crowded Phromthep Cape, this offers excellent views to the south.

**4 Big Buddha Viewpoint**
A religious site, this is home to a massive white marble Buddha statue *(see p82)*.

**5 Khao Khad Viewing Tower**
**MAP K4**
This hilltop tower in Cape Panwa provdes picturesque views, including the Big Buddha statue.

**6 Wat Ko Sirey**
**MAP L3**
On an islet off Phuket's east coast, this temple offers great views over the sea.

**7 Monkey Hill**
Don't get close to the naughty resident macaques on this hill *(see p13)*.

**8 Radar Hill Viewpoint**
**MAP H3**
At 1,735 ft (530 m) above sea level, this is the highest point on Phuket.

**9 Phi Phi Viewpoint**
**MAP M5**
The route is steep but with good steps. It takes about 30 minutes to reach the top.

**10 Helicopter Charters**
This is a breathtaking way to see Phuket from above. A ten-minute flight will cost around B5,000.

# 🔟 Beaches

**Palm-fringed Kata Beach**

### 1 Kata Beach

The seashore here has two separate beaches, Kata Yai and Kata Noi, which are divided by a rocky cliff. Kata Yai is the larger, and busier, of the two. Once a haven for back-packers and hippies, Kata Beach today caters to an increasingly upscale crowd, and is very popular for its stunning beauty *(see pp28–9)*.

### 2 Patong Beach

Phuket's premier nightlife center also offers a long, straight beach, ideal for swimming or jogging away the effects of the previous night's revelry. The beach has something for everyone: toward the south end, parasailing rides and jet skis roar; moving north, there are sunbeds and umbrellas for rent; while the far north end of the beach is the most peaceful *(see pp18–19)*.

### 3 Bang Tao Beach
MAP B6

Home to international windsurfing competitions, Bang Tao is one of Phuket's best places to catch a wave. The upscale Laguna Phuket Resort complex occupies the middle of the beach, while the northern end is undeveloped, offering a respite from the crowds. You can ride horses on the soft golden sand here for a magical experience.

### 4 Surin Beach
MAP A6

Populated by numerous high-end resorts, and with expensive private homes on the surrounding hillside, Surin Beach is sometimes referred to as Millionaire's Row. The beach is very popular with locals, who appreciate the area's excellent seafood. The water is calm and clear from November to April, but be cautious about strong undertows during the low season.

### 5 Long Beach
MAP M6

With some of the best beach-access snorkeling on the Ko Phi Phi islands and with breathtaking views of Ko Phi Phi Leh, Long Beach is both secluded and scenic. During the afternoon, it caters almost exclusively to travelers here; nights are blissfully quiet.

**Long Beach, perfect for snorkeling**

**Secluded Maya Bay**

## 9 Loh Dalum Beach

**MAP L6**

This picture-postcard beach, outlined by green hills and craggy cliffs, is understandably one of Ko Phi Phi's most popular destinations. Swimmers can wade out into its turquoise waters, which, even at quite a distance from the shore, are only waist deep. In the distance, the colored cliffs of Nui Bay rise up against the backdrop of the sky.

## 6 Maya Bay

Perhaps the world's most famous beach after its role in the Leonardo DiCaprio blockbuster *The Beach*, beautiful Maya Bay on Ko Phi Phi Leh has almost single-handedly inspired travelers worldwide to visit southern Thailand. With its sparkling turquoise waters and exquisite white sand – not to mention the near total absence of development – perhaps Maya Bay truly is paradise *(see p100)*.

## 7 Karon Beach

**MAP H4**

This large beach offers plenty of space for sunbathers who want a little privacy. With more than 3 miles (5 km) of powdery white sand lapped gently by the turquoise waters of the Andaman Sea, Karon Beach is often less crowded than its neighbors in Patong and Kata. The magnificent coral reef at its southern end is perfect for snorkeling.

## 8 Mai Khao Beach

Part of Sirinat National Park, Mai Khao Beach is not the usual Phuket tourist beach. There are no private watercraft, and most of the buildings are luxury resorts, none of which infringes on the area's natural beauty. Due to the beach's proximity to the airport, airplanes sometimes fly low overhead *(see p23)*.

## 10 Naiharn Beach

A quiet beach on Phuket's southwestern tip, Naiharn is framed by rolling green hills and emerald waters, and offers a perfect hideaway far from the crowds. The calm, warm water is ideal for swimming, and because there is just one resort property here – the Royal Phuket Yacht Club Hotel, with breathtaking views of the bay – travelers feel as if they've stumbled upon a well-kept secret *(see pp26–7)*.

# 🔟 Scenic Walks

**Waterside walk from Naiharn Beach to Phromthep Cape**

## 1 Naiharn Beach to Phromthep Cape

Walk away from the beach, head clockwise around Naiharn Lake, and follow signs to Phromthep Cape. The hilly, stretching walk will take you past Yanui Beach. At the end of the path are two awesome viewpoints – one facing Naiharn Beach (see pp26–7), and the other, westward over the Andaman Sea.

## 2 Similan Islands

Best known for its exciting underwater sites, the Similan Islands (see pp30–31) also offer a few hiking trails. On Ko Similan, the main island, a tree-lined path winds up to a viewpoint with breathtaking vistas. The best part, of course, is that you'll see hardly a soul on your way up.

## 3 Khao Lak
MAP E2

A number of hiking trails can be found in and around Khao Lak, including a popular scenic forest path starting near the base of the 33-ft- (10-m-) tall Chong Fah Waterfall. Sturdy shoes help while walking the rough jungle trails here. Buddhist monks once kept forest retreats in the area; the ruins of these shelters can still be seen.

## 4 Khao Sok National Park

Trek through ancient forest in Khao Sok (see pp32–5), encountering exotic birds, wildlife, and orchids. Keen bird-watchers will be delighted to see several species of hornbill, while long-tail macaque monkeys and gibbons swing through the trees above. Paddle Asia (see p33) offers a popular soft adventure tour for spotting wildlife, as well as tailored trips.

**Hornbill at Khao Sok**

## 5 Surin Beach to Kamala

From ritzy Surin Beach, home to top-end resort properties, walk south along the sand until you reach a pathway crossing over to Laem Singh Beach. This stunningly picturesque cape on the west coast is tucked between Surin and Kamala. Spend some time here before continuing to Kamala, where there is a relaxed beach and fishing village.

### 6 Chinese Shrines in Phuket Town

A popular way to enjoy the sights of Phuket Town is to focus on its wonderful markets and colorful Chinese shrines. Jui Tui and Put Jaw, two of Phuket's most important Chinese shrines, are located near Ranong Road. This walking tour is marked on the Phuket Town Historical Map, distributed free at Phuket International Airport.

### 7 Mangrove Forests on Mai Khao Beach

At the northern end of Mai Khao Beach *(see p23)* stands one of Phuket's most pristine mangrove forests. An elevated walkway guides visitors above these fascinating trees, which survive in saltwater. Signs describe the plant species here, which include black myrsina, red cycas, and mountain ebony.

**Phuket Town's historic achitecture**

### 8 Historical Architecture in Phuket Town

Take a walk back in time past the classic homes and shops built during Phuket's tin boom in the late 19th and early 20th centuries. Many were constructed in the Sino-Portuguese architectural style. The best routes to take are down Phang Nga, Thalang, Dibuk, Krabi, and Yaowarat roads. Keep an eye out for the spectacular Soi Romanee, located off Thalang Road *(see pp14–15)*.

### 9 Patong

Begin this stroll from the southern end of Patong Beach around dusk *(see p18)*. As you walk up the main beach road, you'll pass by bustling open-air restaurants displaying the day's catch on ice, and lively cocktail-sipping crowds. Turn right onto hedonistic Bangla Road and spend some time simply people-watching.

### 10 Khao Phra Thaeo Royal Forest and Wildlife Reserve

The most popular trek in this national park begins at the park headquarters at Ton Sai Waterfall, navigates through 4 miles (6 km) of virgin forest, and ends at Bang Pae Waterfall. Besides abundant natural plant species, the park is also home to monkeys, flying foxes, wild pigs, and cobras *(see pp20–21)*.

**Lush forests of Khao Phra Thaeo**

# 🔟 **Outdoor Activities**

**1 Tai Chi and Qi Gong**
These ancient Chinese practices, although based on martial arts, are not violent, and more akin to yoga or meditation. Classes are available, but once you're more skilled, you can join the morning sessions in the Suan Luang Park in Phuket town *(see p13)*.

**2 Motorbike Rides**
Cruise the hilly coastal roads of western Phuket, past scenic viewpoints and tropical foliage, on your bike. Motorbikes can be rented in tourist areas and roadside stands sell fuel in old whiskey bottles. Always wear a helmet.

**Rock climbing on Tonsai Tower**

**3 Rock Climbing**
Spidermonkey Climbing: MAP M5; Ko Phi Phi; 0756 1026; www.spidermonkeyphiphi.com
With more than 30 climbing routes, two of which ascend to the 450-ft (137-m) summit, Tonsai Tower on Ko Phi Phi Don also has a number of easy routes which make it ideal for beginners. There are courses on how to belay, lead climb, and multipitch.

**Horseback riding on the beach**

**4 Horseback Riding**
Phuket Riding Club: MAP C5; 60/9 Thepkasattri Road, Thalang; 081 787 2455; www.phuketridingclub.com
Horseback rides on Phuket are a great experience. Mornings and late afternoon are the best time to saddle up, since midday can be very hot.

**5 ATV Touring**
59/26 Moo 5, T. Srisuntorn A. Thalang; 089 874 0055; atvphuket.com
All-terrain vehicles are an exciting way to see local villages, farms, and off-the-beaten-path sights. Phuket ATV Tour includes an option to go white-water rafting in Phang Nga, or to experience a ropes course. Wear sports clothes and closed-toe shoes.

**6 Trekking**
Thailand's scenic jungle paths lead hikers past waterfalls and lush flora, full of wild orchids and ferns. The Khao Phra Thaeo Royal Forest and Wildlife Reserve *(see pp20–21)* has a scenic trail, and at Khao Sok National Park *(see pp32–5)*, walkers can trek through luxuriant jungle and beautiful bamboo forests.

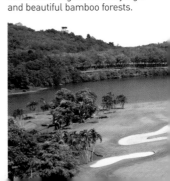

### 7 Cycling
**Amazing Bike Tours Thailand: 087 263 2031; www.amazingbike toursthailand.asia**

Cycling through Phuket's countryside is a great way to explore and to get some exercise while on holiday. Half-day, full-day, and overnight tours through breathtaking scenery also allow cyclists to meet locals.

### 8 Bungee Jumping
**Jungle Bungy Jump: MAP J2; 61/3 Wichitsongkram; 07632 1351; www.phuketbungy.com**

Those seeking an adrenaline fix can plunge down a beautiful lagoon in Kathu's bungee-jumping site. Jungle Bungy offers standard leaps, tandem dives, and touch-water dives. All jumpers are awarded certificates of courage.

### 9 Ziplining
**Hanuman World: MAP J4; 105 Moo 4 Chaofah Road, Wichit; 07639 0189; www.hanuman worldphuket.com**

Safely strapped into a harness and attached to a cable, zipliners sail high above ground propelled only by gravity. Phuket has several zipline providers.

### 10 Golf
Phuket is one of Thailand's top golfing destinations, thanks to its picturesque and challenging courses. The rolling greens of the Blue Canyon Country Club's *(see p92)* two championship courses host a number of professional golf tour events that attract acclaimed golfers.

**Blue Canyon golf course**

## TOP 10 ACTIVITIES FOR RAINY DAYS

**Indulging in a Thai massage**

**1 Cooking Classes**
Learn to make delicious traditional Thai food at one of the island's many local cooking schools.

**2 Thai Massage**
This ultra-relaxing form of massage involves stretching and deep, but not painful, pressure.

**3 Spa Treatment**
With its legendary hospitality, Thailand has earned a reputation as one of Asia's top spa destinations.

**4 Museums**
Phuket's rich tin-mining history can be seen through exhibits at a number of local cultural museums.

**5 Temples**
Visit one of Phuket's 40 Buddhist temples to observe local monks performing traditional ceremonies.

**6 Batik Painting Class**
Visit a batik gallery and create your own version of the popular southeast Asian fabric art.

**7 Shopping**
Rain or shine, the street markets are always open. Phuket has many indoor shopping complexes too.

**8 Phuket Shooting Range**
Indoor and outdoor shooting ranges offer target practice for all ages and abilities.

**9 Cinema**
SF Cinema City, located at Jungceylon in Patong, and the cinemas at Central Festival near Phuket Town, all show the latest releases.

**10 Bowling**
A modern bowling alley with 16 lanes is located at SF Cinema City.

# 🔟 Marine Activities

**Snorkeling in Phuket's azure waters**

### 1 Snorkeling

Almost every beach here has snorkeling opportunities, with boat trips to the popular shallow-water reefs surrounding Phuket. Masks, fins, and snorkels are available at beachfront rental shops.

### 2 Kite Surfing

Kite Boarding Asia: MAP B4; 74/10 Nai Yang Beach (Dec–Mar: MAP J4; Chalong Bay); 081 591 4594; www.kiteboardingasia.com

The northern beaches of Phuket get the best wind for this activity, in which a parachute-like kite pulls the rider on a small surfboard. Since a level of skill is required, it can be more rewarding than parasailing.

**Kayakers at Phang Nga Bay**

### 3 Swimming

A translucent turquoise, delightfully warm, and fringed by soft sand, the Andaman Sea has made Phuket one of the world's favorite destinations. Whether at bustling Patong or idyllic Yanui, Phuket's beaches offer great swimming.

### 4 Deep-Sea Fishing

Phuket Fishing Charters: MAP J4; 48/12 Soi Sunrise, Chalong; 08137 03181; www.phuketfishing charters.com

The Andaman Sea offers anglers a chance to cast for big-game fish, from prized marlins and sailfish to hard-fighting tuna and giant trevally. Most sportfishing off Phuket operates on a catch-and-release policy.

### 5 Scuba Diving

The dive sites here are among the best in the world. With crystal-clear visibility, gorgeous coral reefs and rock formations, and abundant sea life, there are astonishing underwater opportunities for divers.

### 6 Kayaking

Explore Phang Nga Bay's extraordinary sea caves in a kayak or a canoe. Rock tunnels lead into lagoons surrounded by jungles with hornbills, kingfishers, and even monkeys. John Gray's Sea Canoe (see p37) has been leading eco-friendly canoe trips since 1983.

### 7 Surfing

Though not one of the world's main surfing destinations, Phuket's west coast nonetheless offers ample opportunities to catch a wave. Kata and Bangtao beaches host annual surfing and windsurfing competitions. Other surf spots include Kalim, Naiharn, and Surin beaches.

### 8 Parasailing

As the speedboat accelerates, your parachute pulls you up into the sky to enjoy staggering overhead views of emerald waters and green hills. Once the excitement of takeoff is over, you'll soon feel relaxed whilst surveying the scene below.

**Sailing on a Chinese junk**

### 9 Sailing

**Phuket Sail Tours: MAP C5; 199/20 Moo 5, Srisoonthorn, Thalang; 087 897 0492; www.phuketsail tours.com**

Cruise to uninhabited islands with pearly sand beaches, palm trees, and blue waters. Chartered yacht, sailboat, and junk trips offer an opportunity to explore unspoiled locations in the Andaman Sea.

### 10 Phuket Wake Park

**MAP J2 ▪ Phuket Cable Ski, 86/3 Moo 6, Vichitsongkram Road, Kathu ▪ 07620 2527 ▪ Open 9:30am– sundown daily ▪ www.phuketwake park.com**

Since 1997, Phuket's only wake park has given wakeboarders and water skiers a setting to hone their skills, with ramps, kickers, and slide rails.

**TOP 10 BIG GAME FISH IN PHUKET**

**Grouper swimming amongst coral**

**1 Sailfish**
The ocean's fastest fish migrates through waters near Phuket during the summer months.

**2 Yellow Fin Tuna**
These beautiful, powerful fish have long been one of the favorite prey of big-game anglers.

**3 Dogtooth Tuna**
These massive fish dwell near elevated tropical reef pinnacles in the deep waters around Phuket.

**4 Dorado**
Sometimes called mahi-mahi, these surface-dwelling, ray-finned fish are fantastically colorful.

**5 Giant Trevally**
Though not physically huge, the giant trevally puts up one of the toughest fights in the sea.

**6 Wahoo**
The meat of the wahoo, a prized big-game fish, is considered a delicacy by many gourmet cooks.

**7 Spanish Mackerel**
With its razor-sharp teeth, this fish often cuts its way through trolling bait.

**8 Barracuda**
This toothy, ray-finned fish eats almost everything. It is well known for its frightening appearance.

**9 Black Marlin**
One of the most prized captures in the Asia Pacific, the black marlin makes for the perfect trophy.

**10 Grouper**
The biggest grouper ever caught off Phuket, captured with shark bait, weighed nearly 198 lb (90 kg).

*Following pages* Performance at the famous Simon Cabaret at Patong Beach, Phuket

# 🔟 Children's Attractions

**One of Phuket Fantasea's lavish musical extravaganzas**

### 1 Phuket Fantasea

A magical, Disney-like affair, the colorful Phuket Fantasea show thrills young audiences with its carnival games, souvenir shopping street, and exciting parades, pageants, and street shows at the theme park. The enormous Golden Kinnaree Buffet satisfies even the pickiest of eaters. The park has attracted some controversy due to its use of animals for performances (see p82).

### 2 Phuket Trickeye Museum

MAP P5 ▪ Cnr Montri and Phang Nga roads, Phuket Town ▪ 07621 2806 ▪ Open 10am–7pm (last adm 6pm) ▪ Adm ▪ www.phukettrickeyemuseum.com

Over 100 trompe l'oeil sculptures and 3D drawings put visitors in unlikely and hilarious environments, such as balancing on a rickety bridge over a raging river. It's great for photo opportunities.

### 3 Phuket Aquarium

MAP K5 ▪ Sakdidet Road, Cape Panwa ▪ 07639 1126 ▪ Open 8:30am–4:30pm daily ▪ Adm ▪ www.phuketaquarium.org

Set on a scenic bay, this aquarium houses over 150 fresh- and saltwater species, including electric eels, sharks, sea turtles, and stingrays. Displays cover Thailand's rivers, lakes, coral reefs, and mangroves.

### 4 Splash Jungle Waterpark

With twisting waterslides, a wave pool, and the 1,100-ft- (335-m-) long lazy river, this water-theme park (see p94) is excellent. In the Boomerango water slide you will plunge down, through a tube, into the Super Bowl, before hitting the splashdown pool.

### 5 Surf House

Kata Beach: MAP H5, Southern Kata Beach, 08197 97737, Open 10am–midnight daily; Patong Beach: MAP N2, 162/6-7 Taweewong Rd, Open 9:30am–11pm daily ▪ Adm ▪ www.surfhousephuket.com

A high-pressure wave-generating machine throws a shallow sheet of water up a sloping "pool." Beginner

**Catching a wave in the Surf House**

surfers hold onto a guiding safety rope. If they should happen to "wipe out," the strong water flow ensures that, instead of sliding back down, they shoot safely upwards. It's great fun for kids over 10.

### ⑥ Go Karting
MAP H2 ■ Patong Go-Kart Speedway, 118/5 Vichitsongkram Road, Kathu ■ 07632 1949 ■ Open 10am–7pm daily ■ Adm ■ www. gokartthailand.com

With kids' karts reaching speeds up to 25 mph (40 kmph), and specially designed karts driven by an adult with a child's passenger seat, the Patong Go-Kart Speedway often hosts Mini Grand Prix races, including competitions for kids.

**Golfing with dinosaurs at Dino Park**

### ⑦ Mini-Golf at Dino Park
MAP H4 ■ Marina Phuket Resort, Karon Beach ■ 07633 0625 ■ Open 10am–midnight daily ■ Adm ■ www.dinopark.com

This 18-hole miniature golf course navigates around a swamp, lava cave, waterfall, erupting volcano, and a roaring Tyrannosaurus Rex. A fun environment for a competitive round of putting, it also has a theme bar and restaurant.

### ⑧ The Kids Club
MAP N2 ■ 2nd floor, Patong Promenade, 70 Bangla Road, Patong ■ 081 085 0008 ■ Open 10am–9pm daily ■ Adm

The Kids Club offers slides, crawl tubes, swings, a trampoline, a ball room, a flying fox ride, an indoor

soccer pitch, and much more for children of all ages. On duty, there are seven full-time nannies, who assure the play stays fun and safe.

### ⑨ Ghostinium Phuket
MAP J3 ■ 2nd floor, Central Festival Phuket East, Phuket Town ■ 095 491 9800 ■ Open noon–8pm Tue–Sun ■ Adm

An indoor attraction that is good for rainy days, Ghostinium is an animatronics museum, bringing a weird blend of science-fiction future and prehistoric past to life. Consisting of five main rooms featuring about 16 large, fully animated exhibits, it provides fun and education for kids and adults alike, as well as a few surprises and even frights. Visitors under five might find it a bit too scary.

### ⑩ Aqua Zone Marine Park
MAP N2 ■ Patong Beach ■ Open Dec–Apr: 9:30am–6pm daily ■ Adm

Located near Soi Bangla, these 13 inflated floating play stations are housed in a roped-off section of sea protected from motorized marine traffic. The park offers a climbing mountain, trampoline, waterslide, and seesaw.

# 🔟 Entertainment Venues

### 1 Hard Rock Café

MAP P1 ▪ Rat Uthit Road, Patong ▪ 07634 0210 ▪ Open 8:30pm–1:30am for live music▪ Adm

This internationally known establishment is decorated with memorabilia from famous rock legends, and has an excellent line up of performers. The restaurant has the capacity to seat 300 people at once, and along with the bar, is spread over two floors.

**Bangla Road's nightlife scene**

### 2 Bangla Boxing Stadium

The upper deck seats at Bangla Boxing Stadium look straight down at the action, and are close enough that an uppercut glancing off a boxer's jaw might make you leap out of your seat. These are the best seats in the house. Fight promoters cruise through the streets of Patong in pickup trucks during the afternoon, promoting the fights of the day with loud Muay Thai music *(see p18)*.

### 3 Simon Cabaret

MAP N3 ▪ Sirirat Road, Patong Beach ▪ 07634 2011 ▪ Open 7:30–9:30pm daily ▪ Adm ▪ www.phuket-simoncabaret.com

Phuket's most popular cabaret features outrageous costumes and sets, along with a flamboyant cast of transvestite performers. Since 1991, Simon Cabaret has promised male guests they will arrive relaxed but leave confused, because the performers are "more of a man than you'll ever be, and more of a woman too!"

**Flamboyant Simon Cabaret**

### 4 Bangla Road

MAP N2

For people-watching, you won't find a setting more outrageous than the night scene on the infamous Bangla Road. At once seedy and harmless, this central vein of Patong is filled with beer bars, club promoters, and pleasure-seeking travelers from every corner of the globe. The streets coming off Bangla Road are home to even more entertainment venues.

### 5 Phuket Fantasea

A spectacular stage show stars trapeze artists and traditional dancers.There's also a theme park filled with games and shops, all with an elephant theme *(see p82)*.

### 6 Snake Shows

MAP J4 ▪ Phuket Shooting Range, 82/2 Patak Road ▪ 07638 1667 ▪ www.phuket-shooting.com

Watch a deadly cobra have venom extracted from its razor-sharp fangs or a handler kiss one between its eyes. At a Phuket snake show, you can even also have your photograph taken with a massive boa constrictor.

### 7 Phuket Siam Niramit

MAP K2 ■ Chalermprakiet Road, Ratsada, north of Phuket Town ■ 07633 5000 ■ Open 5:30–10:30pm Wed–Mon ■ www.siamniramit.com

A tasteful but lively cultural showcase of the best of Thai classical dance, music, and martial arts, with top-level performers and special effects. The show itself runs from 8:30–10pm, but it's best to arrive early to enjoy the Thai village, and floating market on the grounds. Good for the whole family.

### 8 Patong Boxing Stadium

Phuket's top venue to watch Muay Thai presents real fights every Monday and Thursday night. Foreigners who train at the local gyms frequently get onto the cards against each other, or local Thai boxers, and these fights are often among the most exciting. Early evening fights pit younger, lightweight boxers against one another; the bouts gradually build up toward the main event (see p18).

**Muay Thai, Patong Stadium**

### 9 Fire Dancing

Popular on Ko Phi Phi Don's beaches, and in some of Patong's beachfront hotels, this rare performance art features flaming staffs and poi spinning in the darkness to pulsating music. To watch these glowing rays of light is mesmerizing, and in photographs the fire dancers often appear to be playing with halos.

### 10 Go-Go Bars

Patong, in particular Bangla Road, is well known for its many adult venues. Club promoters stroll the street with programs describing what will be on stage that night. Always use your best judgment when entering any bar, and make sure you ask for prices before ordering.

---

**TOP 10 FILMS SHOT ON PHUKET**

**Scene from *Tomorrow Never Dies***

**1 *The Man with the Golden Gun* (1974)**
This 007 movie featured Ko Khao Phing Kan (see p36), now popularly known as James Bond Island.

**2 *The Killing Fields* (1984)**
Based on Cambodia's Khmer Rouge regime, this movie shows Phuket's French and US embassies.

**3 *Good Morning, Vietnam* (1987)**
Starring Robin Williams and Chintara Sukapatana, this film's jungle scenes were shot on Phuket.

**4 *Casualties of War* (1989)**
Brian De Palma's Vietnam War film features very realistic jungle scenes filmed on Phuket.

**5 *Cutthroat Island* (1995)**
Starring Geena Davis, this pirate film was shot in secluded Maya Bay on Ko Phi Phi Leh (see p100).

**6 *Tomorrow Never Dies* (1997)**
Phang Nga Bay (see p36–7) was portrayed as Vietnam's Halong Bay in this 007 film.

**7 *The Beach* (2000)**
Ko Phi Phi Leh's Maya Bay stole the show in this movie by Danny Boyle.

**8 *Star Wars: Episode III – Revenge of the Sith* (2005)**
Backdrops from Krabi province were featured in this movie.

**9 *The Impossible* (2012)**
Shot and set in Khao Lak, this is based on the true story of a Spanish family caught up in the 2004 tsunami.

**10 *Patong Girl* (2014)**
This follows a German family's visit to Phuket, where the teenage son falls in love with a transgender Thai woman.

# 🔟 Bars and Nightclubs

**Musicians playing a gig at the Timber Hut**

### 1 Timber Hut

Phuket Town's top live music venue features an excellent in-house band. Busy during the week, and sometimes downright wild on weekends, this is a great place to dance and party. A favorite with local Thais, the bar also attracts its fair share of foreign visitors (see p85).

### 2 After Beach Bar

Near Karon Viewpoint, on the winding mountain road between Kata and Rawai, this relaxing bar overlooking the sea plays a constant stream of reggae and acoustic tunes. It's popular for post-beach cocktails while watching the sunset (see p85).

### 3 Rockin' Angels Blues Café

**MAP P4 ■ 55 Yaowarat Road, Old Phuket Town ■ 89654 9654 ■ Closed Monday**

This lively blues venue is run by a Singaporean guitarist. The café and bar may be small, but it is a great place to hang out if you become tired of the blaring dance music heard elsewhere in the town. There are live blues and classic rock performances from the band six nights a week.

### 4 Aussie Bar

Located right in the middle of Bangla Road, Patong's best-known family-friendly sports bar screens all the big football, cricket, and rugby matches on more than 30 TVs. The bar promotes upcoming games on its website (see p85).

### 5 Banana Disco

A long-term crowd pleaser, Banana Disco comes to life around midnight, when crowds flock onto the dance floor for the pounding house music. A great place to dance and drink, the disco remains one of Patong's most popular late-night venues. The B200 cover charge gets you one drink (see p85).

**Selection of drinks, After Beach Bar**

### 6 Z1implex Mixology Laboratory

MAP Q5 ■ Phang Nga Road ■ 084 003 6664 ■ Open 9pm–1am

Unique, friendly, trendy – this Phuket venue is comfortable and cozy, with a DJ that keeps the volume at the right level for conversation.

### 7 Yoonique Stone Music Café

A local favorite, this funky little dive behind Naiharn Lake hosts regular jam sessions and live bands in a unique and artistically decorated environment *(see p85)*.

### 8 Sunflower Bar

MAP M6 ■ Tonsai, Ko Phi Phi ■ Open 11–2am

Sunflower is more relaxed than most Tonsai nightlife. The "buckets" (Thai whiskey, Red Bull, cola and ice, in a plastic bucket) are infamous, but they do nice coconut-based cocktails, too.

**Crowds outside Kangaroo Bar**

### 9 Kangaroo Bar

Centrally located on Bangla Road, Kangaroo Bar draws lively crowds. This popular venue has an in-house DJ, and is also famed as a prime vantage point for scoping out Patong's colorful passersby *(see p85)*.

### 10 Molly Malone's

The island's most popular Irish pub has been going strong since it first opened in 1999. On the main beach road, Molly Malone's offers live pub-rock every night, and flatscreen TVs broadcast live sports. It serves traditional pub fare, as well as brews such as Guinness, Kilkenny, and Magners Cider on tap *(see p85)*.

---

## TOP 10 FAVORITE LOCAL DRINKS

**Singha and Chang beers**

**1 Singha Beer**
Most foreigners pronounce the name of this lager as "Singh-ha," although the proper pronunciation is "Singh."

**2 Chang Beer**
This potent lager is one of the country's top-selling beers. Equally popular on tourist T-shirts is the Chang elephant logo.

**3 Leo Beer**
A flavorful lager, Leo Beer is produced by Boon Rawd Breweries.

**4 Tiger Beer**
Singapore's first locally brewed beer is popular throughout Thailand.

**5 Red Bull Cocktails**
The energy drink's formula was invented by a Thai businessman, who still owns 49 per cent of the company.

**6 "Buckets"**
Be wary of this potent Thai specialty, a mix of alcohol, cola, and Red Bull in a bucket, meant to serve a group.

**7 Sangsom**
Despite its reputation as a Thai whiskey, the liquor is in fact a rum.

**8 Phuket Beer**
The bottle's logo features a brightly colored hornbill, perched near Phuket's Phromthep Cape.

**9 100 Pipers**
This popular western-style whiskey is imported from (although not bottled in) Scotland.

**10 San Miguel Light**
This brew from the Philippines can be found widely throughout Thailand, including Phuket.

# TOP 10 Restaurants

### 1 Silk
A stylish Thai restaurant with contemporary interiors, Silk serves some of the best Thai cuisine in Phuket. The snapper in ginger, celery and pickled plums is a must-try as is the signature dish, the Goon Sarong, with prawns wrapped in Phuket noodles (see p87).

### 2 Boathouse Wine and Grill
This stylish seaside restaurant features a huge wine cellar with more than 800 labels. The excellent French and Thai fusion cuisine competes with classic wine and grill favorites, such as prime meat and chops (see p87).

### 3 On the Rock
Diners could not be closer to the sea at this highly acclaimed restaurant, which is part of the Marina Phuket Resort. Much of the attraction is the ambience created by the views offered thanks to the eatery's position on Karon Beach. Getting a beachfront table, particularly for sunset, often requires a

**Stylish White Box Restaurant**

reservation well in advance. The setting is reflected in On the Rock's seafood menu (see p87).

### 4 White Box Restaurant
With a rooftop lounge with stunning views of Patong Bay, this Mediterranean- and Thai-inspired eatery is popular for cocktails and tapas. In-house jazz musicians, as well as global DJs, entertain diners from 10pm (see p87).

### 5 Thong Dee Brasserie
A top-quality and well-priced restaurant serving international and Thai cuisine. The Khi Mao spaghetti is a creative fusion of Thai and Italian, whilst the Australian tenderloin is a real treat (see p87).

### 6 La Trattoria
This excellent, award-winning Italian restaurant at Dusit Thani Laguna Phuket, a luxury hotel (see p112), serves authentic homemade pastas and other classics from this culinary country. The eatery is set in a stylish area in lush tropical gardens, with fine, Italianate interiors (see p97).

**Entrance to La Trattoria**

### (7) Kra Jok See

Tucked into an 18th-century Sino-Portuguese shop house in Phuket Town, this charming restaurant, with exposed wooden beams and candlelit tables, serves delicious traditional Thai cuisine. However, the night really begins after dessert, when the music is cranked up for one of Kra Jok See's legendary dance parties. Reservations are recommended *(see p86)*.

### (8) Baan Rim Pa

Perched on a cliff above Kalim and Patong bays, Baan Rim Pa serves royal Thai cuisine, once found only in the kingdom's palaces. The emphasis in this cooking is on precise presentation and color, so it requires special training for chefs *(see p87)*.

**Baan Rim Pa's dramatic setting**

### (9) Sala Bua

Located at Impiana Cabana Resort *(see p113)*, this beachfront restaurant features Thai and Pacific-Rim fusion cuisine. The Australian fire-roasted Chateaubriand is recommended *(see p87)*.

### (10) Kopitiam by Wilai

Serving *hokkien mee* (Hokkien fried noodles), a Phuket specialty, this colorful eatery is the younger sibling of the perinnially popular Wilai restaurant. The space has been designed like a Chinese shop house. Other specialties include *phat thai* and southern Thai curries *(see p86)*.

---

**TOP 10 THAI DISHES**

*Khao niaw mamuang* **dessert**

**1 Tom Yum Gung**
Simmered in a clear broth, this hot and sour prawn soup introduces a world of exhilarating new flavors.

**2 Phat Thai**
An iconic Thai street food, this features stir-fried rice noodles, eggs, fish sauce, tamarind juice, and more.

**3 Phat Kraprao**
This spicy, flavorful stir-fry is made with chili and basil leaves, and is often served with rice and a fried egg.

**4 Gaeng Kiaw Wan**
A Thai green curry, this is usually cooked with chicken or beef, and can be spicy and a little sweet.

**5 Gai Phat Met Mamuang**
Chicken stir-fried with cashew nuts is a popular Thai dish, especially in tourist areas.

**6 Somtam**
A spicy salad made from shredded unripened papaya, *somtam* is often eaten with sticky rice.

**7 Tom Kha Gai**
Made with coconut milk, galangal, lemongrass, and chicken, this is a delicious hot soup.

**8 Khao Phat**
A simple dish made of Thai fried rice, *khao phat* is often served with cucumber and sweet chili sauce.

**9 Por Pia**
These Thai spring rolls, usually fried, are often stuffed with vegetables, noodles, and pork or shrimp.

**10 Khao Niaw Mamuang**
Made with succulent fresh mango and sticky rice, this dish is drizzled with a sweet coconut cream sauce.

*For a key to restaurant price ranges see p87*

# 📖🔟 Markets and Shopping Areas

## 1 Jungceylon
MAP P2 ■ Open May–Oct: 11am–10pm daily; Nov–Apr: 11am–11pm daily ■ www.jungceylon.com

Anchored by a department store and a French supermarket, Jungceylon – a massive international mall in Patong – has over 300 shops selling everything from sports clothes to perfumes and luxury cosmetics.

**Exterior space at Jungceylon**

## 2 Central Festival Phuket
MAP J3 ■ Open 10:30am–10pm daily

Central, Thailand's top retailer, runs the biggest and best mall on the island. As well as the department store, there are over 120 outlets, good restaurants and cinemas, and Ghostinium (see p61) for the kids.

## 3 Thalong and Dibuk Roads
MAP P5

These streets in old Phuket Town offer many wonderful shops tucked inside historical buildings selling Chinese embroidery, antiques, wooden figurines, and products from Laos, Cambodia, and Myanmar.

## 4 Phromthep Cape Market
The best souvenirs from this popular viewpoint might be your own photos, but you'll also find a wide range of handicrafts and original art-work in the cape's outdoor markets. Arrive in the late afternoon, before the crowds start pouring in (see p27).

## 5 Naka Weekend Market
This large, open-air bazaar (see p12) sells soaps, candles, sculpture, beachwear, flip-flops, used shoes, and almost anything else you can imagine. It also has dozens of stands selling Thai food.

## 6 Turtle Village Shopping Centre
MAP B2 ■ Open 9am–10pm daily

This upscale shopping center in Mai Khao gives northern Phuket shop-pers a trendy place to buy unique Thai souvenirs. Turtle Village offers luxurious Jim Thompson silk, art-work, jewelry, pearls, and more.

## 7 Kata Plaza
MAP H4

Head here for watches, sunglasses, and beachwear, as well as row after row of quality T-shirts. Bargaining is always possible, sometimes even expected. It's best visited at night; daytime here can be insufferably hot.

## 8 Phuket Town Night Market
MAP P5

With lower prices than in Patong, Kata, and Karon, the night market on Thalang Road, in Phuket Town, offers a similar selection of T-shirts, fishermen's pants, and wood-carvings, as well as second-hand clothes and Thai music albums.

**Patong night market's food stalls**

**⑨ Patong Night Market**

At sundown, vendors throughout Phuket set up makeshift tables and tents to peddle everything from handicrafts to DVDs. Patong's night market in particular turns the entire town into one big, sprawling night bazaar (see pp18–19).

**⑩ Plaza Surin**

MAP A6 ■ Open 9am–8pm daily

For high-end boutiques, visit Plaza Surin's 12 stores, which sell unique items, such as Thai furnishings, original artwork, natural spa products, and cutting-edge audio-visual goods. The upscale Silk (see p66), is a restaurant and bar serving delicious Thai cuisine.

**Phuket Town's lively night market**

## TOP 10 EXOTIC FRUITS IN PHUKET

**1 Mangosteen**
The thick, red skin of this fruit (mang khut) encloses sweet, slightly tart, and creamy white segments inside.

**2 Mango**
No Thai holiday is complete without trying sweet mango (ma muang) with sticky rice.

**3 Lychee**
A major Thai export, the lychee (lin jee) has a thin, hard skin that encloses a thick layer of sweet flesh surrounding a small seed.

**4 Longan**
Covered with a crisp skin, this fruit (lam yai) has sweet flesh that resembles that of a lychee.

**5 Dragon Fruit**
This wonderful pink fruit (geow mangon) is shaped like a flower and has light, sweet, and crunchy flesh.

**6 Durian**
The world's smelliest fruit, durian is not permitted inside some hotels. The creamy yellow flesh inside the spiky shell is considered an acquired taste.

**7 Papaya**
This is a staple fruit in the Thai diet. Try the spicy green papaya salad (som tam) for a fiery experience.

**8 Pomelo**
Somewhat like an Asian grapefruit, this citrus fruit (som oh) features in the excellent Thai salad yam som oh.

**9 Rambutan**
A very interesting-looking fruit, the rambutan (ngo) features a hairy red exterior covering soft, sweet, oval-shaped flesh.

**10 Rose Apple**
This decorative bell-shaped fruit (chompoo) has glossy pink skin, with crisp, juicy, and acidic flesh inside.

**Fragrant, sweet dragon fruit**

# 🔟 Souvenirs

**Interior of Chan's Antique House**

## 1 Antiques

**Chan's Antique House: MAP J2; 99/42, Moo 5, Chalermprakiat, Ratchakan Thi 9 Road; www.chans-antique.com**

The best places for genuine antiques are Soul of Asia (see p95), an art gallery housed in two old Chinese shops, and upscale Chan's Antique House, which offers Phuket's largest collection of art and antiques.

## 2 Seashells

The best place to find rare seashell specimens, or handicrafts made of seashells, is the Phuket Seashell Museum (see p42). The Phromthep Cape market (see p68) also offers a great selection.

## 3 Bespoke Clothing

Phuket's bespoke tailors are commonly found in Patong, Kata, and Karon beaches. Don't wait until the end of your trip; several fittings are needed. They can also copy any garment you bring to the shop. Pay attention to the fabric quality used.

## 4 Local Crafts

**OTOP Shopping Paradise: MAP N2; Rat U Thit 200 Pee Road, Kathu, Phuket**

Revenues from sales are passed directly to the crafts people, so the market provides local and rural artisans with a better income.

## 5 Religious Amulets

**MAP P5**

The best selection of religious items is found in the Amulet Market in the center of old Phuket Town. While mainly Buddhist, Taoist and animist pieces are also on offer, and are taken seriously by aficionados; rare and, supposedly, powerful pieces can fetch prices upwards of B100,000.

## 6 Original Artwork

Artists sell original paintings and reproductions at street-side galleries throughout Phuket. The quality varies, and the costs are always negotiable.

**Vibrant Thai silk cushions**

## 7 Thai Silk

**Jim Thompson: www.jim thompson.com**

Thai silk is not as fine as the Chinese variety, but it is lustrous and hangs well in clothing. The best source is Jim Thompson, named for the American tycoon who revived, and later epitomized, the Thai silk industry. There are six branches on Phuket, including one at the airport.

### 8 Traditional Thai Furniture

MAP J3 ■ Island Furniture: 90/4 Moo 2, Chao Fah West Road ■ 07626 3707 ■ www.islandfurniture-phuket.com

Furniture made of crushed bamboo, recovered teak wood, rattan, water hyacinth, and more can be found in many shops. Island Furniture can recreate pieces from sketches or from photographs.

### 9 Batik Cloth

Although an Indonesian craft, Phuket artisans are now using this wax-resist dyeing technique and incorporating Thai artistic motifs. Cloth and items made from it are easy to find in boutiques and night markets. Look for the government-sponsored OTOP brand pieces.

**Colorful Thai Batik cloth for sale**

### 10 Pearls

MAP K1 ■ Phuket Pearl Factory: 58/2 Moo 1, Tambon Kohkaew ■ 07623 8002 ■ www.phuketpearl.com

White, black, or cream pearls, produced on local pearl farms, can be found in Phuket's markets. You can see how pearls are cultured and extracted at Naka Noi island, off the northeastern coast.

**Farmed pearls being selected**

---

**TOP 10 BARGAINING TIPS**

**Market traders, Phuket**

**1 Have fun**
Approach your shopping experience lightheartedly – you'll enjoy yourself all the more.

**2 Smile**
A smile goes a long way with local salespeople.

**3 Don't Lose Your Head**
Don't let your negotiations get too serious, and never raise your voice – it's taboo in Thailand.

**4 Be Patient**
Don't buy something from the first stall you visit. In Phuket, you'll almost always see it again.

**5 Compare Prices**
Get price quotes from different vendors selling the same goods; occasionally one vendor's prices are much lower than the others.

**6 Buy In Bulk**
Sellers often reduce their prices substantially if you buy more than one item.

**7 Politely Ask For Discounts**
The initial asking price is often about twice as high as the seller's final settling price.

**8 Walk Away**
The classic strategy is to politely say "No, thank you," and walk away. The vendor will often stop you and accept the price you offered.

**9 Use Your Head**
Avoid too-good-to-be-true prices, especially for expensive items such as gemstones or antiques.

**10 Currency Exchange**
Memorize your exchange rate so you can quickly calculate the cost in your home currency.

# TOP 10 Phuket for Free

**Celebrating the Vegetarian Festival**

## 1 Festivals and Sporting Events

It seems there's always some sort of festival or sporting event taking place on the island (see pp74–5), and most of them are free, whether it's to watch and join in the goings on, or to cheer on the participants, such as at the Vegetarian Festival.

## 2 Bangla Road at Night

The main drag of Patong Beach comes alive in a blaze of neon and raucous music after dark. Since so many of the bars are open-air, it's easy to soak up the buzz and people-watch in comfort (see p62).

## 3 Phromthep Cape Sunset

At the southernmost tip of the island, narrow Phromthep Cape juts into the sea, and provides a spectacular view at sunset. There's a lighthouse on the cape with a small museum (free admission). The cape is popular with group tours, and those with their own transport can seek more isolated spots above Yanui Beach, a short distance north of the cape (see p48).

## 4 Wat Chalong

Phuket's largest and most popular temple, located in the island's southeast, attracts both visitors and the Buddhist devout. Located in the base of the Grand Pagoda, the murals depicting events in the life of the Buddha are a highlight (see pp16–17).

## 5 Monkey Hill

Just to the east of Phuket town, Monkey Hill, also known as Khao To Sae, offers excellent viewpoints, a Taoist shrine, and a population of macaques who are quite used to being offered food. They are great fun to watch, but afford them the respect you would any wild animal. The hill is also popular with fitness enthusiasts – the road is closed to vehicular traffic after 5pm, making it ideal for a sunset run. There's a small fitness park as well (see p13).

**Macaque, Monkey Hill**

## 6 Karon Viewpoint

Located up in the hills south of Kata Beach, Karon Viewpoint has superb views over both Kata beaches and Karon. Several shaded pavilions provide great spots for a picnic (see p29).

**Sunset vistas from Karon Viewpoint**

## 7 Buddhist Meditation Classes

MAP J4 ▪ 69/509 Soi Chaofah 5, Chalong ▪ 08727 97655 ▪ Classes: 11am Tue, 7pm Thu ▪ www.phuket-meditation.com

A free introductory lecture and class in the practice of Buddhist meditation is offered by the Phuket Meditation Center. Longer courses and retreats are also available.

## 8 Big Buddha

Clad in gleaming white marble, this 148-ft- (45-m-) tall statue rests atop a hill near Wat Chalong and commands panoramic views of the island. It cost over 100 million Baht to construct, financed by donations from the faithful (see p82).

**Opulent interior of a Chinese shrine**

## 9 Phuket Town Chinese Shrines

The faiths of Taoism, Mahayana Buddhism, and Confucianism have a vast pantheon of deities and spirits, to which these shrines pay homage. Visitors are welcome, but should remove shoes before entering and observe the decorum that these sacred places deserve (see pp46–7).

## 10 Khao Rang Fitness Park

Located just north of Phuket Town, and famous for its viewpoints and good restaurants, Rang Hill (see p13) also offers a free outdoor fitness park with a variety of exercise devices such as inclined planes for sit-ups. The walk up to the park is a good warm-up.

---

**TOP 10 BUDGET TIPS**

**Shoes on sale in a street market**

**1** Buy a local SIM card for your phone or tablet. These are available from shops selling phones as well as most convenience stores. Data speeds are quite good.

**2** Charming as they look, avoid using tuk-tuks, which tend to take you to stores run by the driver's friends or family. Use metered taxis, or rent a car or motor scooter.

**3** The cheapest beach resort accommodation on the island is to be found in the Kata Beach hostels.

**4** Eat in shopping-mall food courts. These are just above street stall price, but offer air-conditioned comfort.

**5** Use budget airlines (Air Asia, Thai Smile) when flying in from Bangkok or elsewhere in the region.

**6** Try Airbnb rentals for upscale accommodations at a much cheaper rate than the resorts.

**7** Bargaining is appropriate for any non-food item in a street market. Start with half the vendor's stated price and keep smiling.

**8** Imported alcoholic drinks are taxed up to 300 per cent here, but the local beers (Singha, Leo, Chang) are good, as is the rum – try SangSom with soda and a squeeze of lime.

**9** Traditional massage parlors don't offer the luxury found in upmarket spas, but these ubiquitous shops provide a good body or foot massage at a reasonable price.

**10** Look for shops displaying a "VAT refund for tourists" sign, and claim the 7 per cent tax back on your purchases when you leave Thailand.

# 🔟 Fairs and Festivals

### 1 Chinese New Year
**Late Jan/early Feb**

Celebrated with firecrackers, crashing cymbals, and colorful costumes, the Chinese New Year marks the beginning of a new lunar year, and is an auspicious day for the Chinese. The holiday is especially important in Phuket Town, where people dress in bright red costumes, and numerous parades and feasts are held.

**Bang Neo Shrine at Chinese New Year**

### 2 Old Phuket Festival
**Late Jan/early Feb**

Chinese opera, rickshaw rides, and a Phuket Baba Light Show are a few of the highlights of this festival, which coincides with the Chinese New Year. The festival is held in Phuket Town on Thalang, Krabi, and Phuket roads.

### 3 Phuket Gay Pride Festival
**Feb**

Established in 1999, this festival includes four nights of wild parties and parades in Patong. With cabaret shows, fashion shows, and more, this annual event seeks to create a stronger gay, lesbian, bisexual, and transgender community on Phuket.

### 4 Phuket Food and Music Festival
**Feb/Mar ■ MAP B5 ■ www.lagunaphuket.com**

This popular festival is held at the Laguna complex of hotels and villas. Attracting a huge audience, it has a varied line up of musicians, with performances ranging from jazz to country music. Apart from the music, there are different food stalls and treats.

### 5 Songkran
**Apr 13–15**

The traditional Thai New Year celebration turns the entire country into one big water fight. Getting sprayed with water is considered good luck, and many Thais visit temples to pay respect to Buddha by sprinkling water on his statue.

### 6 Visakha Puja
**May**

Thailand's Buddhist temples overflow with merit-makers on this holy day marking the birth, enlightenment, and death of the Buddha – three events that occurred on the same day in different years. At night, believers walk around the temples in a candlelit procession.

**Dazzling street parade marking the Phuket Gay Pride Festival**

**Por Tor Festival**
Aug

During the annual "Hungry Ghosts" festival, offerings of special cakes, candles, and flowers are made to deceased ancestors, who are believed to revisit their earthly homes on this day. Chinese shrines serve as the center of the festival.

**Lion dancer at the Por Tor Festival**

 **Phuket Vegetarian Festival**
Late Sept/early Oct ▪ www.phuket vegetarian.com

This nine-day festival serves to "purify" participants and bring them good health, but has nothing to do with food. At Chinese shrines in Phuket Town, fire walking, and extreme acts of body piercing and self-mortification take place.

 **Loy Krathong**
Late Oct/early Nov

Sins of the previous year float away, as Thais pay homage to the guardian spirit of water. Small banana-leaf vessels are decorated with flowers and candles. If a person's boat floats, they will enjoy good luck for the year.

 **Chao Ley Boat Floating Festival**
Nov

At this festival, participants float ceremonial vessels hoping to receive happiness and prosperity, and ward off bad luck. Held in Chao Ley (sea gypsy) villages, the festival also pays tribute to the Chao Ley's ancestors.

**TOP 10 SPORTING EVENTS**

**1 Muay Thai**
No visit here is complete without witnessing this martial art form.

**2 The Bay Regatta**
Feb
More relaxed than the King's Cup, these races are popular with visitors.

**3 Phuket Bike Week**
Apr
This festival involves music, parties, and awesome motorbikes.

**4 Phuket International Cricket Sixes Tournament**
Apr
This brings international cricketers into competition in Karon.

**5 Phuket International Rugby Tournament**
May
The three-day tournament draws teams from Australia and Asia.

**6 Laguna Phuket International Marathon**
Jun
The marathon starts at Bang Tao Beach.

**7 Cape Panwa Hotel Phuket Race Week**
Jul
A week of parties and yacht races, this festival attracts many participants.

**8 Phuket Surfing Contest**
Sept
At Kata Beach, this contest lets surfers vie for more than B100,000 in prizes.

**9 Laguna Phuket Triathlon**
Nov
A 1-mile (2-km) swim, 34-mile (55-km) cycle race, and 8-mile (13-km) run.

**10 King's Cup Regatta**
Dec
The regatta began in 1987, to mark HM King Bhumibol's 60th birthday.

**Surfer, Phuket Surfing Contest**

# 🔟 Day Trips

### 3 Ko Khai Nok
MAP F3

Another great snorkeling destination, this island has coral reefs hugging its coastline – the prime underwater attraction. Brilliantly colored parrot-fish can often be spotted. The small swimming cove features white sand flanked by rocky headlands. Vendors sell fresh coconut water from huts.

### 4 Ko Yao Yai and Ko Yao Noi
MAP F3

These picturesque islands in Phang Nga Bay feature charming thatched-roof homes and rubber plantations, interspersed with vast tracts of lush foliage. Most of the accommodations are on Ko Yao Noi, the smaller of the two islands. You can hire a kayak from your hotel to explore the beautiful rock formations facing the island. Alcohol is generally not sold here, except within hotel premises.

**Beachfront at Ko Yao Yai Island**

### 1 Ko Kaew
MAP H6

A Buddha statue greets visitors to this small island, which is visible from Phromthep Cape. A replica footprint of the Buddha makes this a holy pilgrimage site for some monks. On the island's far coast is another Buddhist shrine and *chedi* (stupa).

### 2 Ko Racha
MAP E4

Made up of two islands, Ko Racha is a renowned diving and snorkeling site. Ko Racha Yai has a few bunga-lows and restaurants, and a pretty beach. It's a great place for star-gazing. Smaller Ko Racha Noi is less developed, with rockier shorelines.

**Ko Racha Yai beach**

**Breathtaking Ko Phi Phi**

### 5 Ko Phi Phi
MAP L4–M6

A speedboat from Rassada Port can whisk you to these islands in an hour, after which you can visit Maya Bay on Koh Phi Phi Leh, Monkey Beach, and some of the smaller islets nearby. The trip includes a stop for lunch on Ko Phi Phi Don. You'll catch an astonishing sunset from the stern on your way back to Phuket for dinner.

### 6 Ko Rang Yai
MAP L1

Home to the Phuket Pearl Farm, this private island cultivates three types of pearls for export. Ko Rang Yai also offers outdoor activities, including camping, mini-golf, and an air-gun shooting range. Visitors can watch demonstrations on how pearls are cultured, harvested, and turned into jewelry. The guides also explain how to tell the difference between real and fake pearls.

### 7 Ko Bon
MAP J6

A 15-minute boat ride from Rawai Beach, this small rocky island features a crescent-shaped beach

along the west coast. The beach has a quaint restaurant that serves seafood, Thai, and Western dishes. The island's east coast is owned by Evason Resorts and is for the exclusive use of their guests.

### 8 Ko Maphrao
MAP L2

Boasting magnificent deserted beaches and coves, Ko Maphrao (its name means Coconut Island) is just five minutes by boat from Phuket's east coast. Popular activities here include swimming, snorkeling, and exploring the coastline's mangrove forests by boat. There's only one hotel, but the island also offers homestays with local families.

**Ko Tapu limestone pillar**

### 9 Ko Khao Phing Kan

Ever since *The Man with the Golden Gun* was filmed here, few people have referred to this island as Ko Phing Kan (see p36). Now widely known as James Bond Island, it is one of Phuket's most popular day trips. The famous limestone rock called Ko Tapu, or Nail Island, juts out of the sea nearby.

### 10 Ko Hae
MAP J6

Just 2 miles (3 km) off Phuket's southeastern shore, Ko Hae, or Coral Island, is a pretty island surrounded by colorful coral reefs. The island has two long sandy beaches – Long Beach and Banana Beach. The most popular activity here is exploring the vast Staghorn coral reefs, located around 328 ft (100 m) offshore.

# Phuket
# Area by Area

White-sand beach on Koh Miang in
the Similan Islands National Park

# ᴛᴏᴘ10 The South

Of the five million tourists who visit Phuket annually, the majority flock to Patong, Karon, and Kata on the island's southwest coast. Here, they find an array of world-class restaurants, activities, and hotels, all set amid the tropical backdrop of rolling green hills and crystal-blue waters. But most of southern Phuket, with its busy beaches, seaside restaurants, open-air bazaars, and throbbing nightclubs, doesn't aim to be an escape. Phuket Town, with its historical architecture, Chinese heritage, and southern Thai cuisine, is almost wholly distinct from Phuket's bustling tourist areas.

**Statue at a Chinese shrine, Phuket Town**

## AREA MAP OF THE SOUTH

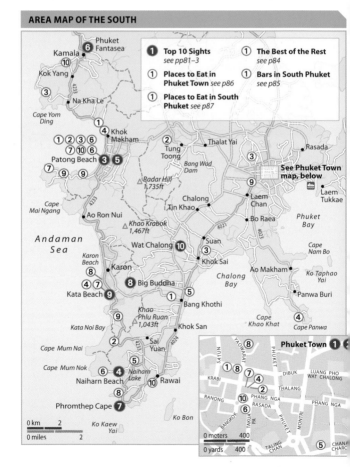

| ① | Top 10 Sights see pp81–3 | ① | The Best of the Rest see p84 |

| ① | Places to Eat in Phuket Town see p86 | ① | Bars in South Phuket see p85 |

| ① | Places to Eat in South Phuket see p87 | | |

### 1 Phuket Vegetarian Festival

Dating back to the 1820s, the Phuket Vegetarian Festival originated in Kathu after members of a Chinese opera contracted a fatal disease and sought ways to purify themselves and please the gods. For most visitors, the highlight of this entertaining nine-day event are the bizarre acts of piercing and self-mortification practiced by participants, who plunge spears through their cheeks, walk across burning-hot coals, and perform other gruesome displays of self-sacrifice (see p13).

### 2 Phuket Town

The capital of Phuket province, Phuket Town offers everything from world-class beaches and scenery to 100-year-old Straits Settlements mansions and shop houses, traditional open-air markets and shops, as well as the vividly hued Chinese shrines built during the tin boom of the late 19th and early 20th centuries. Walking tours are the best way to explore (see pp12–15).

**Tranquil Patong Beach**

**Historic street in Phuket Town**

### 3 Patong Beach

This area is more relaxed these days, following the government clean-up campaign (see p83). There are fewer hawkers, and motorized watercraft are only allowed in some areas, but there is a scarcity of sunbeds. The island's best dining can be found along the waterfront, with top restaurants commanding impressive views. The legendary nightlife in Patong needs little introduction. It runs the gamut from pulsating dance clubs to cabaret shows and open-air bars, along with the adult venues ablaze in neon lights (see pp18–19).

### 4 Naiharn Beach

A picturesque bay on Phuket's far southwestern coast, Naiharn (see pp26–7) remains one of the island's better-kept secrets. With just one beachfront resort, the landscape doesn't feel at all encroached upon. Tall screw pines populate the area behind the beach, providing a buffer between the nearby Buddhist monastery and Naiharn Lake. Charming Naiharn Town is a short motorbike or car ride from the beach, but is well worth a visit for its coffee shops and art studios.

### 5 Muay Thai

Two venues in Patong host regular bouts in which south Thai fighters pummel one another with elbows, shins, knees, and fists. Patong Boxing Stadium and Bangla Boxing Stadium (see p18) witness plenty of vicious knockouts. The music accompanying the fights sounds like something composed in a madhouse – a haunting windpipe, tribal drums, and tiny finger cymbals. Foreign fighters come to train at the Muay Thai gyms here, and they often test their mettle in the rings.

**Fireworks at Phuket Fantasea**

### 6 Phuket Fantasea

MAP G1 ■ 99 M3 Kamala Beach Kathu ■ 07638 5000 ■ Open 5:30pm–11:30pm Fri–Wed ■ Adm ■ www.phuket-fantasea.com

This lively theme park is enough like Disneyland for kids to love it, and enough like Las Vegas for parents to enjoy it too. It is packed with fun activities, entertainment, and even shopping. The spectacular Fantasy of a Kingdom is the longest-running live show in Asia. Before this dazzling show, you can enjoy one of Asia's largest buffet dinners in the 4,000-seat dining facility at the Golden Kinnaree restaurant.

### 7 Phromthep Cape

On clear nights, a west-facing hilltop on Phuket's southern tip feels like a large public gathering in anticipation of what could be a space shuttle launch or a fireworks show, with all eyes trained on the horizon. However, there is no such spectacle – the crowds are simply here to witness the end of the day, and nature's show is indeed a spectacular one (see p27).

### 8 Big Buddha

MAP H4 ■ Open 8am–7:30pm daily

This dramatic religious monument perched on top of Nakkerd Hill has become one of Phuket's iconic landmarks and attracts hundreds of visitors each day. The 148-ft- (45-m-) tall, cross-legged white marble Buddha makes an awesome sight when viewed from sea level, and offers even greater appeal from the hilltop, from where visitors can enjoy sweeping views and pleasant breezes. There's also the chance to enjoy a sunset dinner at Nakkerd Sea View Restaurant.

### 9 Kata Beach

Increasingly upscale, Kata draws positive reviews for the way in which it harmonizes its tropical beauty with ever-growing crowds and infrastructure. Indeed, the beach here offers many of the same joys as Patong, such as parasailing and jet-skiing, yet it retains a decidedly more relaxed feel. At night, Kata has enough restaurants and nightlife to

**Phromthrep Cape's magnificent view**

**THE GREAT PHUKET CLEAN-UP**

A crackdown on corruption was one of the reasons the Thai military gave for seizing power in May 2014. Their first major target was the island of Phuket. Illegal beachfront buildings were bulldozed, taxi licenses enforced, jet-ski rentals curtailed, and the clutter of beach furniture removed. The reaction from visitors has been very favorable.

feel like it's got a pulse, but it isn't overbearing. With a wide selection of shopping, both on the beach and off, it's easy to see why Kata's popularity endures (see pp28–9).

**Shrine in Wat Chalong**

## ⑩ Wat Chalong

The island's most famous Buddhist temple is located about 4 miles (6 km) south of Phuket Town. Wat Chalong features a number of brilliantly colored buildings, including a glittering pagoda that was added to the complex in 2002. The temple has long been important as, during an uprising of migrant tin workers in 1876, the local Siamese fled here for protection, where two monks offered them shelter and helped resolve the dispute peacefully. Today, many Thais visit the statues of Luang Pho Chaem and Luang Pho Chuang in the temple's sermon hall to seek their blessings (see pp16–17).

**EXPLORING PHUKET'S SOUTHWEST COAST**

### ▶ MORNING

After hiring a car, start your journey in **Patong** (see p81), the tourist center of the island. Follow the road signs for Highway 4233 towards Karon, Kata, and Phromthep Cape. This coastal road takes you to the island's southern tip. Make your first stop at **Karon Beach**, one of Phuket's largest tourist beaches. Buy a coconut from a beach vendor and enjoy the fresh, sweet water inside. Continuing south on the road, you will pass the shop-lined streets of **Kata**. Stop if something catches your eye. After **Kata Noi**, the road starts to ascend a steep hill that winds its way up to the famous **Karon Viewpoint**, from where you can enjoy breathtaking views and take fabulous photographs, so bring your camera. Continue to **Naiharn**, where a delicious seaside lunch awaits you under the shade of umbrellas and casuarina trees behind **Naiharn Beach** (see p81).

### AFTERNOON

After a relaxed lunch, follow the road signs to **Phromthep Cape**. You'll drive around **Naiharn Lake**, and then up and down a hilly, tree-lined road. At the bottom of the hill is **Yanui Beach**, a charming place to swim, snorkel, and relax under the trees. The road then continues to Phromthep Cape, with its magnificent views over the Andaman Sea. Just be sure to reverse course and reach Patong before it gets too dark. The journey takes about 45 minutes, and you don't want to be on these roads at night.

See map on p80 ←

# The Best of the Rest

### ① Phuket Orchid Farm
MAP J4 ▪ 67/1 Soi Suksan 1, Viset Road, Chalong ▪ 07628 0226 ▪ Open 9am–5:30pm daily ▪ www.phuketorchids.com

This heavenly nursery and greenhouse displays over 1,500 types of orchid.

### ② Karon Viewpoint
With breathtaking views of the island, this viewpoint is usually populated with vendors selling drinks, snacks, or photo opportunities with exotic birds (see p29).

**Phuket Orchid Farm**

### ③ Chalong Bay Rum Distillery
MAP J4 ▪ Soi Palai, Chaofah Road, Chalong ▪ 093 575 1119 ▪ Open 10am–8:30pm Mon–Sat (tours: 2–6pm, hourly)

The hand-crafted white rum made here is distilled from sugar cane juice rather than molasses. The price of a tour includes a mojito.

### ④ Phuket Aquarium
Part of the Phuket Marine Biological Center, this aquarium introduces visitors to an enchanting underwater world with stingrays, sharks, and sea turtles (see p60).

### ⑤ Chinese Shrines
The colorful shrines scattered throughout the island play an important role during the Phuket Vegetarian Festival (see pp46–7).

### ⑥ Ao Sane Beach
This rugged, secluded little beach, not far from Naiharn, offers great opportunities for snorkeling and has a peaceful vibe (see p27).

### ⑦ Paradise Beach
MAP G3 ▪ Adm

Not far from the often crowded Patong Beach, this delightful little stretch emanates tranquility with its soft sand and palm trees; there is a coral reef not far off shore.

### ⑧ Yanui Beach
This lovely cove (see p26) – an ideal setting for kayaking, snorkeling, or reading a book under the shade of palm trees – is located just past the windmill visible from Naiharn Beach.

### ⑨ Emerald Beach
MAP G3

Thanks to its exposed location, this 1,640-ft- (500-m-) long beach, called Hat Tri Tra in Thai and tucked away south of Patong, offers a quiet place to hide out and work on your tan.

### ⑩ Rawai Beach
MAP H6

A non-swimming beach, Rawai is known for its seafood restaurants along the beach. Speedboats and long-tail boats can be chartered at Rawai to visit some of the smaller islands nearby.

**Long-tail boats at Rawai Beach**

# Bars in South Phuket

**1** ### Kangaroo Bar
MAP N2 ■ Bangla Road, Patong
■ Open early afternoon–2am daily

This vibrant venue on Bangla Road plays thumping rock music, and has a free barbeque about once a week.

**2** ### Molly Malone's
MAP N2 ■ 94/1 Thaweewong Road, Patong ■ 07629 2771 ■ Open 9am–2am daily

This spirited Irish pub features live music every night.

**3** ### Roots Rock Reggae Bar
MAP P3 ■ Nanai Road, Patong ■ 087 271 4656 ■ Open 1pm–2am daily

With regular barbeque and live music parties, this funky little reggae bar in Patong also features a small shop selling handmade jewelry, leather bags and belts, and more.

**4** ### Artspace Café and Music Bar
MAP H5 ■ 7 Ket Kwan Road, Kata ■ 090 156 0677 ■ Open 11–1am daily

This bar has a cool bohemian vibe, with lots of plants and sculpture. It's a friendly place with a loyal following of visitors and locals. There's great food and live music every night.

**5** ### Yoonique Stone Music Café
MAP H6 ■ 14/61–62 Sai Yuan Road, Rawai Beach ■ Open 6pm–2am daily

An eclectic spot, this café features live music and regular theme nights. Jam sessions on Tuesdays and live bands on Fridays regularly draw large, enthusiastic crowds.

**6** ### Aussie Bar
MAP N2 ■ Bangla Road, Patong ■ Open 9:30am–2am daily

If you want to catch a live sports game, the Aussie Bar, which broadcasts sporting events from all over the globe, is your best bet.

**7** ### Rock City
MAP N2 ■ 169 Rat-U-Thit 200 Pee Rd ■ Open 8pm–2am daily

A lively venue, Rock City hosts top local and international bands playing classic rock, heavy metal, grunge, and more. There is no cover charge if you arrive before 11pm.

**8** ### Timber Hut
MAP P5 ■ Yaowarat Road, Phuket Town ■ 07621 1839 ■ Open 9:30pm–2am daily

The house band here is considered one of the best on Phuket. There is a dance floor and seating upstairs.

Caribbean stylings at After Beach Bar

**9** ### After Beach Bar
MAP H5 ■ Highway 4233 ■ 081 894 3750 ■ Open 9am–11pm daily

A wooden structure with a laid-back, Caribbean vibe, After Beach Bar is located near Karon Viewpoint and specializes in cocktails, seafood, and spectacular sunset views.

**10** ### Banana Disco
MAP N2 ■ Beach Road, Patong ■ 07634 0301 ■ Open 9pm–4am daily

This is one of Phuket's oldest discos. The high-energy house music played into the early hours here draws hordes of late-night revelers.

*See map on p80*

# Places to Eat in Phuket Town

### 1 Dibuk Grill and Bar
**BB**

Serving authentic Thai and French cuisine, and offering a full selection of fine wines, this elegant restaurant (see p14) is set inside a traditional Straits Settlement house.

**China Inn Café and Restaurant**

### 2 China Inn Café and Restaurant
**BB**

The magnificent exterior of this shop house (see p15) gives way to a leafy courtyard, where diners can enjoy remarkable Thai and Western cuisine, and delightful Thai desserts.

### 3 Thungkha Kafae
MAP N4 ▪ Top of Rang Hill ▪ 07621 1500 ▪ Open 11am–10pm daily ▪ B

Atop Rang Hill, this outdoor café enjoys lovely views and a reputation for the best iced coffee on Phuket.

### 4 Kopitiam by Wilai
MAP P5 ▪ 18 Thalang Road, Phuket Town ▪ 083 606 9776 ▪ Open 11am–10pm daily ▪ B

With an old-fashioned feel and photographs of Phuket in bygone eras, Kopitiam is owned by the same family that runs Wilai next door.

### 5 Laemthong Seafood
MAP Q6 ▪ Chana Charoen Road ▪ 07622 4349 ▪ Open 11am–10pm daily ▪ B

The oldest Chinese eatery on Phuket is popular for its seafood and Chinese cuisine, including oyster omelets, and Peking chicken.

### 6 Kra Jok See
MAP P5 ▪ 26 Takua Pa Road, near Rasada Circle ▪ 07621 7903 ▪ Open 6pm–midnight Tue–Sun ▪ B

Served in a charming old shop house, the fixed-price dinner is followed by dancing and a cabaret show. It's a full-evening experience for which reservations are required.

### 7 Wilai Restaurant
MAP P5 ▪ Thalang Road ▪ 07622 2875 ▪ Open 7am–2pm daily ▪ B

A selection of pre-cooked curries and stir-fries is served at this popular spot. *Penang Moo* (coconut milk curry with pork) is highly rated.

### 8 Ran Jee Nguat
MAP P5 ▪ Corner of Yaowarat and Dibuk roads ▪ Open 10am–8pm daily ▪ B

This Chinese-run restaurant serves one of the island's best-loved local specialties – *kanom chine naam ya phuket* (Chinese noodles in a puréed fish and curry sauce).

### 9 Roti Chao Fa
MAP N5 ▪ Chao Fa Road ▪ Open 6am–noon daily ▪ B

Delicious curries served with flat bread and exotic teas make this a popular choice for breakfast.

### 10 Anna's Café
MAP P5 ▪ Rasada Road ▪ 07621 0535 ▪ Open 6pm–midnight Mon–Sat ▪ BB

This restaurant serves upscale Thai food family-style. The *massaman* (beef curry) and *gaeng som* (sour curry) are two favorite dishes here.

# Places to Eat in South Phuket

## 1 White Box Restaurant
MAP H2 ■ 247/5 Prabaramee Road, Kalim Beach ■ 07634 6271 ■ BBB

The restaurant features both Thai and international dishes with a setting adjacent to the Andaman Sea.

## 2 Thong Dee Brasserie
MAP J2 ■ Soi Bangthong 110/25, Kathu ■ 07631 9323 ■ Open 4–10pm Tue–Sun ■ BB

A reasonably priced restaurant offering Thai and international cuisine. The Thai delicacies are from different regions of the country. Do try the *kaeng pod* (spicy red curry).

## 3 Diavolo Restaurant
MAP G1 ■ Paresa Resort, 49 Moo 6, Layi-Nakalay Road, Kamala Beach ■ 07630 2000 ■ Open 8am–11pm daily ■ BBB

Generous à la carte breakfasts and Italian delicacies for lunch and dinner are served here.

**The interior of Diavolo Restaurant**

## 4 Baan Rim Pa
MAP H2 ■ 223 Prabaramee Road, Kalim Beach ■ 07634 0879 ■ Open 1–11pm daily ■ BBB

This restaurant is famed for its Royal Thai Cuisine and views of Kalim Bay.

## 5 Kan Eang
MAP J4 ■ 9/3 Chofa Road, Chalong Bay ■ 07638 1323 ■ Open for lunch & dinner daily ■ BB

On Phuket's eastern coast, Kan Eang serves classic Chinese-Thai seafood.

## 6 Sala Bua
MAP N1 ■ 41 Thaweewongse Road, 83150 Patong ■ 07634 0138 ■ Open 6am–midnight daily ■ BBB

Imaginative East-West fusion dishes, with a focus on seafood, served up at a spacious and breezy beachfront location *(see p67)*.

## 7 Boathouse Wine and Grill
MAP H5 ■ 182, Koktanode Road, Kata Beach ■ 07633 0015 ■ Open 6:30am–11pm daily ■ BBB

Known for its spectacular wine list, this beachfront restaurant serves French and Thai dégustation menus.

## 8 On the Rock
MAP H4 ■ 47 Karon Road, Marina Phuket, Karon Beach ■ 07633 0625 ■ Open noon–10pm daily ■ BBB

This beachside restaurant, specializing in Thai and international seafood, is open for lunch, as well as dinner.

## 9 La Gritta
MAP N1 ■ Amari Coral Beach Resort, Patong Beach ■ 07634 0106 ■ Open 11am–midnight daily ■ BB

In a quiet bayside setting, this Italian restaurant specializes in gourmet pizzas and handmade pastas.

## 10 Silk
MAP G1 ■ Andara Resort & Villas, Kamala Beach ■ 07633 8777 ■ Open 7am–10pm daily ■ BBB

This restaurant is part of the Andara Resort, offering international cuisine coupled with a stunning view of the sea from Kamala Beach.

*See map on p80*

# TOP 10 The North

Virgin rain forest, mangroves, wildlife sanctuaries, and unspoiled golden-sand beaches where giant leatherback turtles return each year to lay their eggs – northern Phuket abounds in opportunities to connect with the area's magnificent natural surroundings. Jungle trekking trails, a half-buried golden Buddha statue, and picturesque swimming coves comprise natural and historic wonders, while theme parks, golf courses, and tree-top canopies also attract many visitors. The beaches north of Kamala offer more privacy, tranquility, and access to nature for those who seek a little more space – and less bustle – during their holiday on Phuket.

**Wat Prathong**

## AREA MAP OF THE NORTH

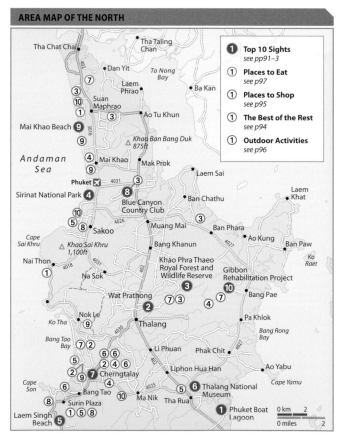

1 **Top 10 Sights**
see pp91–3

1 **Places to Eat**
see p97

1 **Places to Shop**
see p95

1 **The Best of the Rest**
see p94

1 **Outdoor Activities**
see p96

*Previous pages* The iconic Big Buddha statue atop Nakkerd Hill

**Rows of glamorous yachts moored at the Phuket Boat Lagoon**

### (1) Phuket Boat Lagoon
MAP K1 ■ 22/1 Moo 2
Thepkasattri Road ■ 07623 9055
■ www.phuketboatlagoon.com

Luxury yachts from around the world are moored in the lagoon and up-scale marina here. Opened in 1994, the Phuket Boat Lagoon features more than 150 units with restaurants, retail outlets, and sport complexes. The Boat Lagoon Resort has 300 guest rooms, exceptional restaurants, tennis courts, swimming pools, and a Thai spa.

### (2) Wat Prathong
MAP C5 ■ Highway 402
■ Open 8am–5:30pm daily

The half-buried golden Buddha image here draws worshippers and curious tourists alike. Built in the 1750s, Wat Prathong has received many high-profile visitors, including King Rama V in 1909. The statue was most likely half buried as a result of flooding. The reclining gilded Buddha is another popular attraction. The colorful temple complex also features a museum that houses assorted historical items, such as tin-mining tools and Javanese daggers, among others.

### (3) Khao Phra Thaeo Royal Forest and Wildlife Reserve

Home to numerous protected animal species, as well as rare and exotic plant life, this virgin rain forest has a number of jungle trekking trails, two lovely waterfalls, and a gibbon rehabilitation facility. Declared a wildlife sanctuary in 1969, Khao Phra Thaeo contains an especially rare palm species, found only here and called the white-backed palm, which was only identified in 1929. Animals include barking deer, gibbons, and flying foxes, as well as snakes and wild pigs *(see pp20–21)*.

### (4) Sirinat National Park

The pristine shoreline along Phuket's northwestern coast is protected by Thailand's national park service. Every winter, massive sea turtles lay their eggs in the sand here, while virgin mangrove forests can be found at the northern end of the park. A 2,625-ft- (800-m-) long wooden walkway has been built over the mangroves and is a popular scenic walk. The Sirinat National Park protects the pristine Mai Khao, Nai Yang, and Nai Thon beaches, which are a world apart from the raucous party beaches *(see pp22–3)*.

**Coastline of the Sirinat National Park**

### 5 Laem Singh Beach
MAP G1

This beautiful, hidden beach, populated by lush palm trees and giant rocks, feels like a secret cove. However, despite being hidden away from the road, and the fairly steep path required to reach it, Laem Singh beach remains a popular destination throughout the year and becomes especially busy during high season. The rocky areas in the water provide excellent snorkeling opportunities, while the rustic wooden beach restaurants offer tree-shaded spots in which to enjoy fresh seafood.

### 6 Thalang National Museum
MAP D6 ▪ Thalang ▪ 07631 1025 ▪ Open 8:30am–4pm daily ▪ Adm ▪ www.nationalmuseums.finearts.go.th

In 1785, two Siamese women helped defend Phuket against an attack by Burmese soldiers (see pp40–41). For their bravery, they were honored with this museum, and the Heroines' Monument (see p43). A large 9th-century statue of Vishnu, the Hindu god, stands in the museum's main hallway, while other displays feature the island's tin-mining history, its sea gypsy communities, and more.

**SEA TURTLES**

During the November to February breeding season, giant sea turtles, including the magnificent leatherback, return to the northwestern beaches of Phuket – to the same place they were born – to lay their eggs. Mai Khao and Nai Yang beaches provide perfect nesting sites where sea turtles can lay their eggs and bury them in the sand for protection until they hatch.

**Palm-fringed Bang Tao Beach**

### 7 Horseback Rides on Bang Tao Beach
MAP B6 ▪ Open 9am– 5:30pm daily ▪ Adm

Visitors can ride horses from the Phuket Laguna Riding Club on the beautiful golden sands of Phuket's second-longest beach. The experience provides marvelous photo opportunities, as well as being adventurous, as the horses walk, trot, or canter through the calm waters and past stunning scenery. Everyone is catered for – from regular riders to novices, who are well looked after by experienced guides – and all equipment is provided.

### 8 Blue Canyon Country Club
MAP C3 ▪ 165, Moo 1 Thepkasattri Road, Thalang ▪ 07632 8088 ▪ www.bluecanyonclub.com

Golf aficionados rave about Blue Canyon's rolling fairways, towering trees, and exceptionally well-kept greens. The two picturesque championship courses here, the Canyon and the Lakes, are premier golfing destinations. The Canyon Course has hosted the Johnnie Walker Classic three times, playing host to a number of acclaimed golfers. The 17th hole on the Canyon Course is considered one of the 500 best in the world, according to Golf Magazine. Non-golfers will enjoy the club's spa and fine dining facilities.

### 9 Mai Khao Beach

Part of Sirinat National Park, this 6-mile- (10-km-) long beach (see p23) has undulating golden sand lined by palm trees and pines. Development in the area has been limited, resulting in resorts that truly respect the surroundings. The sea can be rough in summer, but the beach makes for an excellent scenic trek, and walkers often find themselves alone with the birds.

### 10 Gibbon Rehabilitation Project

Established in 1992, this center seeks to rehabilitate captive white-handed gibbons and reintroduce them into their natural habitat, while striving to end their illegal use as tourist attractions and pets. You can pay a small donation to adopt a gibbon that has been mistreated in captivity (see pp20–21).

**Gibbons at the Rehabilitation Project**

**A DAY IN NORTHERN PHUKET**

▶ **MORNING**

Hire a private car for this itinerary if you don't have a rented one, since the journey covers quite a bit of ground. Also carry sturdy shoes, swimwear, and a towel. Start the day auspiciously by making merit at **Wat Prathong** (see p91), where local Buddhists revere the half-buried golden Buddha image. The temple is located quite far inland, so it isn't as crowded as Wat Chalong. Continue eastward to the nearby **Khao Phra Thaeo Royal Forest and Wildlife Reserve** (see p91), one of the last remaining habitats for exotic animals on Phuket. Here, park your car near **Bang Pae Waterfall** (see p94) and eat at one of the restaurants near the car park. Better still, buy a take-away meal and enjoy a picnic in the shade near the waterfall.

**AFTERNOON**

A short walk from the Bang Pae Waterfall stands the small **Gibbon Rehabilitation Project**, where gibbons who have been ill-treated in captivity are gently reintroduced into a wild habitat. After watching these fascinating creatures from the viewing platform, you can adopt a baby gibbon for a small amount of money and ensure that the animal continues to receive vital care. If you're feeling energetic, hike the 5-mile- (8-km-) long jungle path to **Ton Sai Waterfall**. When it's time for a bite to eat, visit the floating restaurant located in the coastal mangrove swamps, which are also a protected area. Return to your hotel by the early evening.

See map on p90 ⬅

# The Best of the Rest

### ① Nai Thon Beach
MAP A4

A sleepy little hideaway, this beach is usually free of large tourist crowds. The reefs are popular with divers.

### ② Laguna Phuket Golf Club
MAP B6 ▪ 34 Moo 4, Srisoonthorn Road, Cherngtalay ▪ 07632 4350 ▪ www.lagunaphuket golf.com

Voted one of the best resorts in Asia, this golf club features scenic lagoons and immaculate greens.

### ③ Cable Jungle Adventure Phuket
MAP C5 ▪ 232/17 Bansuaneramit, Moo 8, Srisoonthorn Road ▪ 081977 4904 ▪ Open 9am–6pm daily ▪ www.cablejunglephuket.com

With 15 stations and a 3,937-ft- (1,200-m-) long zipline run, this is a great treetop canopy adventure.

### ④ Wat Mai Khao
MAP B3

A serene and unadorned temple in a quiet forested area near Mai Khao village, Wat Mai Khao also has a bird sanctuary within its compound.

### ⑤ Heroines' Monument
MAP C6 ▪ Thepkasattri Road

Located at the Tha Rua roundabout, this monument is a tribute to the sisters who helped defend Phuket from invaders in the 18th century.

### ⑥ Windsurfing in Bang Tao
MAP B6

Bang Tao enjoys the reputation of being one of Phuket's best places to windsurf. Boards and sails can be rented from local resorts and shops.

**Water gushing at Bang Pae waterfall**

### ⑦ Bang Pae and Ton Sai Waterfalls

The two waterfalls in Khao Phra Thaeo Royal Forest and Wildlife Reserve, linked by a hiking trail, are picturesque destinations surrounded by beautiful jungle scenery *(see p20)*.

### ⑧ Surin Beach
MAP A6

This beach houses some of Phuket's top-end resorts such as The Chedi. The area's wealth is reflected in the neighboring homes and restaurants.

### ⑨ Splash Jungle Waterpark
MAP B3 ▪ 65 Moo 4, Mai Khao Soi 4, Mai Khao Beach ▪ 07637 2111 ▪ Open 10am–6pm daily ▪ www.splashjungle waterpark.com

With thrilling rides, this theme park is an ideal place to splash around.

### ⑩ Nai Yang Beach
MAP B4

A popular picnic destination for locals, this tree-lined beach has restaurants that serve a selection of delicious seafood.

**Sailing boats on Bang Tao beach**

# Places to Shop

**1** **Fine 9 Design**
MAP A6 ■ Surin Plaza, 5/50 Moo 3, Cherngtalay ■ 07624 1141
Enormous shells, vases, ceramic bowls, Thai-style teak wood rattan furniture, and original artwork are available at this upscale home products store at Plaza Surin.

**2** **Jim Thompson**
MAP B6 ■ Canal Village, Laguna Phuket Resort, Bang Tao ■ 07630 4536 ■ www.barufashion.com
The famed silk retail shop has a well-stocked outlet in this smart shopping center. Apart from silk, leather goods and ceramics can also be found here.

**3** **Red Coral**
MAP B2 ■ Turtle Village, Mai Khao Beach ■ 07631 4811
This boutique sells necklaces, photo frames, postcards, beach sandals, bags, and more. The unique seashell and pearl products make great gifts and souvenirs.

**4** **Lemongrass House**
MAP B5 ■ 10/2 M.1, T. Cherngtalay, A.Thalang ■ 07632 5501 ■ www.lemongrasshouse thailand.com
With some 90 aromas to choose from, the spa products sold here are among the best in Asia. Customers can even blend their own products.

**5** **Lola**
MAP A6 ■ Surin Plaza, 5/50 Moo 3, Cherngtalay ■ 07627 1141
A sophisticated boutique, Lola offers high-end designer jewelry and chic accessories, such as scarves, beaded bags, shoes, and clothing.

**6** **Heritage Collection**
MAP B6 ■ 106/19–20 Bang Tao Beach Road, Cherngtalay ■ 07632 5818
Antique wood and bronze Buddha images from southeast Asia along with Chinese sculptures, imperial clothing, and furniture are part of the Heritage Collection.

**7** **Banyan Tree Gallery**
MAP B6 ■ Laguna Phuket Resort, Bang Tao ■ 07636 2300 ■ www.banyantreegallery.com
Showcasing indigenous handicrafts (home furnishings, apparel, candles, jewelry) by artisans from around the world, this gallery seeks to conserve traditional crafts and skills.

Handicrafts at Banyan Tree Gallery

**8** **Soul of Asia**
MAP B6 ■ 5/50 Moo 3, Cherngtalay ■ 07627 1629 ■ www.soulofasia.com
Serious collectors of art will be delighted by this massive collection.

**9** **Canal Village**
MAP B6 ■ Laguna Phuket Resort, Bang Tao ■ www.laguna phuket.com/canalvillage
An outdoor mall of 40 shops, offering clothing, jewelry, sports equipment, and local products, plus restaurants and cafés.

**10** **The Palace of Art**
MAP A6 ■ 103/3 Moo 4, Banbangjoe ■ 07627 3533
This showroom displays some of the best examples of genuine Thai, Myanmar, and Cambodian fine art.

See map on p90 ←

# Outdoor Activities

**Snorkelers enjoying Phuket's crystal-clear waters**

### 1 Snorkeling
There are many opportunities to see beautiful underwater coral formations and colorful schools of fish in and around Phuket. In winter, the clear waters off Surin, Nai Yang, and Nai Thon make for great dives.

### 2 Canoeing
Go canoeing in the incredible mangrove forests and sea caves along Phuket's northeastern and northwestern coasts.

### 3 Golfing
MAP B6

Some of Phuket's best golf courses can be found in the north. Mission Hills, Blue Canyon, and Laguna Phuket offer picturesque, challenging, and well-maintained courses.

### 4 Trekking
Northern Phuket's most scenic trek covers 4 miles (6 km) of jungle trails in the Khao Phra Thaeo Royal Forest and Wildlife Reserve. Guides can be hired at the visitor center near Bang Pae Waterfall (see p94).

### 5 Kite Surfing
With good year-round winds, Phuket's west coast is ideal for kite-surfing enthusiasts. Nai Yang Beach, which is free of speedboats and jet-skis, has a popular kite school that offers classes for beginners. From December to March, the school is based at Chalong Bay (see p56).

### 6 Horseback Riding
The Phuket Laguna Riding Club and Phuket Riding Club offer horseback rides along the seashore at Bang Tao Beach (see p92).

### 7 Ziplining
Soar through the jungle canopy safely harnessed and clipped to a cable that runs from one station to the next. It's an adrenaline rush, but take the time to focus on the beauty of the surroundings as well (see p21).

### 8 Cycling
A bicycle tour is a great way to experience northern Phuket's back roads and trails. Popular trips involve cruising through stunning scenery past villages and plantations in the island's northeast. Cycling trips can last either half a day, a full day, or overnight (see p55).

### 9 Camping
MAP B3

Visitors can pitch a tent on parts of Nai Yang and Mai Khao beaches in the Sirinat National Park. The park's visitor center, at the southern end of Mai Khao, rents out camping gear.

### 10 Swimming
Excellent swimming beaches stretch from Kamala to Mai Khao, on Phuket's northwestern coast. Be cautious during the rainy season, however, as undertows and currents can be strong. Look out for red flags.

# Places to Eat

### 1 Sala Phuket
MAP B2 ▪ 333 Moo 3, Mai Khao Beach ▪ 07633 8888 ▪ BBB

This resort's beachfront restaurant offers fresh seafood, traditional Thai delicacies, and international fare.

### 2 Siam Supper Club
MAP B5 ▪ Tinlay Place, Laguna Phuket, Cherngtalay ▪ 07627 0936 ▪ BB

This has the feel of a gentlemen's club. The Thai and European foods are often innovative, and always excellent. The bar is an expat hang-out.

### 3 Jakajan Seafood Restaurant
MAP B2 ▪ Soi 5 Mae Khao 6 ▪ 81891 3731 ▪ B

Fresh seafood is served up in a casual, Thai-style environment at Jakajan.

### 4 Tatonka Restaurant
MAP B6 ▪ 382/19 Moo 1, 34 Lagoon Road Cherngtalay ▪ 07632 4349 ▪ BB

Influenced by Mediterranean, Asian, and Latino cuisines, the fusion fare receives high praise. Try the sashimi spring rolls and Peking duck pizza.

### 5 La Trattoria
MAP B6 ▪ Dusit Thani Laguna ▪ 390 Moo1, Srisoontorn Road, Cherngtalay ▪ 07636 2999 ▪ BBB

Located in an elegant resort, this retaurant specializes in Italian cuisine, and has good options for vegetarians. The locally caught sea bass and tiger prawns are particularly good.

### 6 Toto Italian Restaurant
MAP B6 ▪ Near Laguna Phuket Resort entrance ▪ 07627 1430 ▪ BB

Traditional Italian dishes, including a wide range of homemade pastas, fresh seafood, meats, and good wood-fired pizzas, make this restaurant a popular choice.

### 7 Kin Dee Restaurant
MAP B2 ▪ 71/6 Moo 5, Mai Khao Beach ▪ 082 814 8482 ▪ BB

Try the crabmeat stir fried with curry powder at this seafood restaurant.

### 8 Black Ginger
MAP B6 ▪ Slate Resort Nai Yang Beach ▪ 07632 7006 ▪ BBB

Situated in a Thai style pavilion on a lake within the upscale Slate Resort, this place has a lovely ambience and serves superb Thai cuisine.

360° Restaurant at twilight

### 9 360° Restaurant
MAP B6 ▪ The Pavilions Phuket, 31/1 Moo 6, Cherngtalay ▪ 07631 7600 ▪ BBB

On a hilltop at The Pavilions Phuket, this romantic eatery is known for its tuna tartar, smoked pork back ribs, and dark chocolate fondue.

### 10 Cucina
MAP B2 ▪ JW Marriott, 231 Moo 3, Mai Khao Beach ▪ 07633 8000 ▪ BBB

An award-winning Italian restaurant at Mai Khao Beach, this trattoria serves authentic rustic cuisine in an unbeatable ambience.

See map on p90 ←

# 🔟 Farther Afield

Try to imagine the perfect tropical landscape, and you will probably conjure up almost exactly the scenery that surrounds Phuket – unspoiled white-sand beaches, enchanting underwater worlds, ancient rain forests, and dramatic limestone cliffs. There are also hundreds of exotic birds, rare plants and flowers, native animals, colorful coral reefs, and awe-inspiring vistas. Easily accessible from Phuket as day trips, southern Thailand's natural wonders draw millions of visitors each year, but at their farthest reaches – when trekking on jungle trails, immersed in the azure sea, kayaking in cave grottoes, or boating through sparsely populated bays – you'll often find yourself alone.

**Junk in Phang Nga Bay**

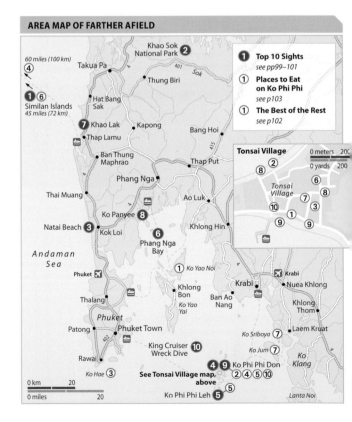

**AREA MAP OF FARTHER AFIELD**

1 **Top 10 Sights**
see pp99–101

1 **Places to Eat on Ko Phi Phi**
see p103

1 **The Best of the Rest**
see p102

**Similan Islands coral reef**

### 1 Similan Islands

One of the world's premier scuba diving destinations, the Similan Islands *(see pp30–31)* offer underwater landscapes renowned for their staggering colors and marine life. The most popular dive sites include East of Eden, Richelieu Rock, and Anita's Reef, where exotic seascapes abound. Located in the Andaman Sea, about 31 miles (50 km) from Khao Lak, the Similans are best visited as part of an overnight or multiday tour. Non-divers can enjoy snorkeling, boat tours, and visits to uninhabited islands.

### 2 Khao Sok National Park

Home to exotic wildlife, such as the Malaysian tapir, wild boars, and pig-tailed macaque monkeys, this national park is one of Thailand's most pristine virgin rain forests. The majestic scenery features deep valleys, towering limestone cliffs, lakes, and jungle paths. Adventures into the park often include elephant treks, canoeing, and jeep safaris. Picturesque Cheow Laan Lake, framed by verdant cliffs, is home to floating bamboo-raft houses, and the area is a favorite with photographers and bird-watchers *(see pp32–5)*.

### 3 Natai Beach
MAP E2

On the mainland just north of Phuket Island, Natai is perfect for anyone seeking an easily accessible hideaway. A 20-minute drive from the airport (closer than some beach areas), it is totally devoid of jet-skis, speedboats, or beach-bed vendors. Accommodation is mainly upscale, although there are also budget options, too. This is Phuket as it was in years long gone by.

### 4 Phi Phi Viewpoint
MAP M5

Enjoy breathtaking views of the sunrise from Ko Phi Phi Don's highest point *(see p101)*, some 610 ft (186 m) above sea level. With first light, the island's dumbbell shape can be seen beyond the treetops, as well as the dramatic rock formations on the far side of the island. The trip to the summit doesn't take much time or effort – it's just 20 minutes or so from Loh Dalum Bay.

**Limestone pillars in Cheow Laan Lake, Khao Sok National Park**

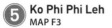

**Maya Bay's hideaway location**

## 5 Ko Phi Phi Leh
MAP F3

Framed on three sides by steep limestone cliffs, and caressed by calm crystal blue waters, the breathtakingly picturesque Maya Bay (see p51) on Ko Phi Phi Leh is best known for its appearance in the Hollywood movie, *The Beach*. Day tours provide lunch at Maya Bay; there are no hotels on the island, but tour companies offer sleepaboards just offshore.

### ECO CONTROVERSY

While *The Beach* was being filmed on Ko Phi Phi Leh in 1999, environmentalists claimed that filmmakers damaged Maya Bay by clearing coconut trees and grass, and altering sand dunes in order to make the beach appear more attractive. The tsunami in 2004, however, essentially washed away all signs of human tampering.

## 6 Phang Nga Bay

Dramatic limestone cliffs jut up from this bay (see pp36–7), providing extraordinary scenery for boat cruises, kayak journeys, and island tours. To experience the bay fully, spend an entire day here, venturing beyond the popular tourist sites such as Ko Phing Kan and Ko Panyee. Kayak tours explore cave tunnels that open into fantastic *hongs* (lagoons). Traditional Chinese junk boats, long-tail boats, and speedboats can be hired along Phuket's east coast piers, as well as from Chalong and Rawai Beach.

## 7 Khao Lak
MAP E2

Pristine jungles hug the coastline, while the clear waters and white-sand beaches of Khao Lak offer a natural paradise for those seeking tranquillity. A number of fascinating diving and snorkeling sites, hidden beaches, and upscale resorts populate Khao Lak. The Khao Sok Lam Ru National Park features beautiful sea cliffs, estuaries, and mangroves. Treks and long-tail boat trips can be arranged at the park's visitor center. The 2004 tsunami devastated Khao Lak, but the area has made a strong recovery, and today tourism is flourishing again.

## 8 Ko Panyee
MAP F2

Most of this small island consists of a massive limestone outcrop that rises vertically out of Phang Nga Bay. The main attraction here is the stilt village constructed in the shallow waters along the island's south side. The island's economy today relies increasingly on day-trippers from nearby Phuket. Fresh seafood restaurants line the shore, and a mosque towers over the village. Visitors often visit Ko Panyee and Ko Phing Kan combined as part of a packaged tour.

## ⑨ Ko Phi Phi Don
**MAP M5**

Once populated by fishermen, and later home to vast coconut plantations, this beautiful island southeast of Phuket is now a thriving tourist destination. With colorful bays framed by cliffs and turquoise waters, Ko Phi Phi Don possesses physical beauty but also has a thriving nightlife and many convenience stores. Although the 2004 tsunami destroyed much of Ko Phi Phi Don, it has now been almost entirely rebuilt.

**Ko Phi Phi Don's main street**

## ⑩ King Cruiser Wreck Dive
**MAP F3**

On May 4, 1997, a ferry on a trip from Phuket to Ko Phi Phi collided with a reef pinnacle and sank. The crew and passengers were all rescued. Today the sunken cruiser remains a popular and relatively uncomplicated dive site, reachable with standard scuba gear. The ship features large openings that offer easy access to the boat's interior *(see p36)*.

**Rugged Ko Panyee island**

### DAY TRIP TO KO PHI PHI

> **MORNING**

Set your alarm clock for early in the morning, and catch the boat that leaves **Rassada Port** on Phuket's east coast at 8:30am. Choose a tour company that arranges pickups from your hotel. Onboard the passenger ferry to **Ko Phi Phi**, you can breakfast on coffee, sandwiches, and fresh fruit on the open-air roof deck or in an air-conditioned cabin. After dropping off some travelers at **Ko Phi Phi Don**, the boat continues to the nearby **Ko Phi Phi Leh** and the world-famous **Maya Bay**. Renowned for its gorgeous beaches, emerald waters, and towering cliffs, the bay is very popular with visitors. You can go snorkeling here before visiting other beautiful bays. Visit **Viking Cave** *(see p102)*, where swifts build "saliva nests," used for making the delicacy known as bird's nest soup. For lunch, the boat returns to Ko Phi Phi Don, where a Thai and international cuisine buffet awaits.

**AFTERNOON**

After lunch, relax on the famous twin bays of **Tonsai** and **Loh Dalum**. These beaches have sun beds with umbrellas, while the comfortably warm blue waters remain quite shallow even quite a long way from the shore. You can also visit **Monkey Beach** *(see p102)*, home to many of these curious creatures. It also offers good snorkeling and opportunities to see colorful fish and coral. Dine at your hotel – to get back in time, take the ferry on its return to Phuket around 4:45pm.

*See map on p98* ←

# The Best of the Rest

### 1 Ko Yao Noi
MAP F3

Popular for its eco-friendly homestay programs, Ko Yao Noi remains an idyllic and rustic destination in Phang Nga Bay. Visitors appreciate its quiet beaches, slow-paced lifestyle, picturesque hiking trails, and kayaking.

### 2 Fire Shows, Ko Phi Phi
MAP F3

Flaming staffs and twirling fiery orbs create a tribal feel during the nightly fire shows on the beach on Ko Phi Phi Don.

Fire show performer, Ko Phi Phi

### 3 Ko Hae (Coral Island)
MAP J6

Nicknamed for the impressive coral reef surrounding the island, this day-trip destination off Phuket's east coast has two pristine beaches.

### 4 Surin Islands National Marine Park
MAP E2

Most easily accessed from Khao Lak, this chain of islands spans nearly 58 sq miles (150 sq km) of underwater area. Pristine under water reefs make this a popular destination for divers.

### 5 Viking Cave
MAP F4

This cave, at Ko Phi Phi Leh, has ancient carvings resembling Viking-style vessels. These petroglyphs confirm the legends of Viking boats visiting the Andaman coast.

### 6 Camping on the Beach at Ko Similan
MAP D2

The tent campgrounds on Ko Similan allow visitors to spend a night on the beach, listening to the waves and watching the sky ablaze with stars.

### 7 Ko Jum and Ko Si Boya
MAP F3

This adjacent pair of secluded islands, boasting great beaches, sea caves, and snorkeling, is reached from the Ko Phi Phi islands by speedboat in an hour. Once home only to sea gypsies, they have very little tourist infrastructure beyond guesthouses – and therein lies the attraction.

### 8 Loh Dalum Beach
MAP M6

This splendid tropical beach on Ko Phi Phi Don features limestone cliffs encircling a white-sand beach.

### 9 Nightlife on Ko Phi Phi
MAP F3

Many people visit Ko Phi Phi for the natural beauty of the islands. Another major draw is Ko Phi Phi Don's legendary nightlife, which includes everything from cocktail buckets and beach bars to fire dancing.

### 10 Monkey Beach
MAP L5

While some come to Ko Phi Phi Don to take photographs of the pesky monkeys on the beach, others come for the snorkeling opportunities at the fabulous reef located offshore.

Monkeys on the beach

# Places to Eat on Ko Phi Phi

## PRICE CATEGORIES

For a three-course meal for two with half a bottle of wine (or equivalent meal), taxes, and extra charges.

**B** under B500 **BB** B500–1,000
**BBB** over B1,000

### 1 Pee Pee Bakery
MAP L6 ■ Tonsai Village ■ Open 7am–5pm daily ■ B

This popular breakfast spot serves fresh doughnuts, pastries, and coffee, as well as decent Thai and Western food.

### 2 Blue Lagune
MAP M5 ■ Ao Nang ■ 098 345 4514 ■ Open 11am–10pm daily ■ B

Peaceful Ao Nang on the island's east coast is home to this gem. It has an unassuming exterior, but inside you'll find great Thai food, friendly service, and reasonably priced seafood.

### 3 Unni's Restaurant
MAP M6 ■ Tonsai ■ 081 979 2865 ■ Open 8am–midnight daily ■ B

An informal but comfortable place, Unni has Western specialties that include great burgers, Mexican food and Greek salads. It's a popular spot for a hearty breakfast.

### 4 Carpe Diem
MAP M6 ■ Eastern Tonsai ■ Open 8–2am daily ■ BB

Located at Phi Phi Village Resort, this beachside eatery serves Thai and Western favorites. At night, Carpe Diem goes into party mode with cocktail buckets and fire shows.

### 5 Jasmine Restaurant
MAP L5 ■ Laem Tong Beach ■ 081 894 1246 ■ Open 10am–10pm daily ■ B

Visit the quiet northern tip of the island for the charmingly unpretentious Jasmine. It's not fancy cooking, but the Thai and Italian food served here is delicious.

### 6 Cosmic
MAP M6 ■ Tonsai ■ B

Delicious pizzas from a wood-fired oven, homemade pastas, and Thai food attract hungry hordes to this popular restaurant.

**Characterful interior of Cosmic**

### 7 Pum Restaurant and Cooking School
MAP M6 ■ Tonsai ■ 081 521 8904 ■ Open 11am–9pm daily (classes from 1:30pm) ■ www.pumthaifoodchain.com ■ B

Not only can you eat delicious Thai food here, but you can also learn how to make it in the cookery school.

### 8 Papaya
MAP M6 ■ Tonsai ■ 091 157 2007 ■ Open 11am–2pm daily ■ B

Run by a former Muay Thai boxer, this popular place serves mouthwatering curries, *somtam* (spicy papaya salad), and *pad thai* (stir-fried rice noodles).

### 9 Song's Pad Thai
MAP M6 ■ Tonsai ■ 084 846 3921 ■ Open noon–11pm daily ■ B

Customers' compliments are written on note pads and affixed to the walls of this popular spot for *pad thai*.

### 10 Le Grand Bleu
MAP M6 ■ Tonsai ■ 081 979 9739 ■ Open 6:30–11pm daily ■ BB

Serving excellent French cuisine and with a decent wine list, this upscale restaurant has an elegant ambience that receives high praise.

*See map on p98*

# Streetsmart

Beautifully restored Sino-Portuguese
shop house in old Phuket Town

# Getting To and Around Phuket

## Arriving by Air

**Phuket International Airport** (HKT) receives daily direct flights from Australia, North America, Europe, and throughout Asia. International big-name and budget airlines as well as charter flights compete with the national carrier, **Thai Airways**, so there is quite a choice. An even greater number of flights arrive at Phuket from destinations within Thailand, including Surat Thani, Bangkok, Chiang Mai, Ko Samui, Utapao (Pattaya), Udorn Thani, and Hat Yai. Airlines include **Air Asia**, **Nok Air**, and **Bangkok Airways**. The flight from Bangkok to Phuket takes only about 90 minutes.

Phuket International Airport is located in the northern part of the island, about 30 minutes' drive from Phuket Town, or an hour from the major southern beaches. The mainland beaches in Phang Nga province north of Phuket, such as Khao Lak, are even closer.

## Arriving by Sea

Passenger ferries, water taxis, speedboats, and private charters arrive at the **Rassada Port** from Ko Phi Phi, Krabi, Trang, Ko Lanta, and Ko Lipe. There is also an international ferry to/from Langkawi Island in Malaysia, with connections to Penang. Cruise liners also call in at Phuket. Rassada Port is just a ten-minute taxi ride away from Phuket Town.

## Arriving by Road

The short Sarasin Bridge links Phuket island with the mainland. There are frequent buses to all major towns in Thailand. Buses between Bangkok and Phuket take around 12 hours. Buses coming from the north circumvent Bangkok (the journey from Chiang Mai takes 20 hours). Reclining "VIP" seats on buses offer you the most comfortable ride. Minivans also run between Phuket and other cities in Thailand, but the bus is preferable for safety and comfort.

Long distance buses arrive at **Phuket Bus Terminal 2**, located 3 miles (5 km) north of town. From here there are connections by various modes of transport to every part of the island. The closest train station to Phuket is in Hat Yai, an 8-hour bus ride or a 30-minute flight away from Phuket.

When considering a bus trip, compare prices with the budget airlines – depending on the season, the bus is not always the best value, although it is certainly more scenic.

## Getting Around by Taxi

Metered taxis are easy to find at the airport, but elsewhere they are few and far between, so it is essential to negotiate a fare in advance. Near major taxi stations, signboards will display a list of the maximum fares to a range of destinations, but still verify the fare with the driver.

The **Airport Authority of Thailand (AOT)** has a limo service, which operates from the airport at a fixed rate. **Grab Taxi** has a convenient app. A government crackdown on illegal taxis has made the situation better, but it's still important to avoid pressure from drivers – don't be rushed into a cab, and make sure that the fare is clearly understood. If you meet a driver you like, get their cell phone number and call them when you need a lift.

## Getting Around by Songthaew

An inexpensive way of traveling between towns, the *songthaew* (literally "two rows") has a row of center-facing benches running down each side of a pickup truck. Rides start from about B20 per person for short distances. Journeys from Phuket Town to various beaches cost about B50–100 per person. They can also be chartered to any destination, and will wait to take you back.

## Getting Around by Minivan

These are similar to a *songthaew*, but they are not open air, ply more fixed routes (such as the Phuket Bus Terminal to all the beaches), don't stop for passengers to get off and on as frequently as a *songthaew*, and cannot be chartered. The routes and stops are not always clear, but your hotel staff can advise you.

## Getting Around by Tuk-Tuk

Unlike in Bangkok, where the tuk-tuk is ubiquitous, these familiar three-wheeled vehicles are no longer used on Phuket. However, small red trucks with open sides, almost like a miniature *songthaew* are often referred to as tuk-tuks. As they tend to be not much cheaper than a taxi, and drivers may take you to tourist traps belonging to friends, it's better to avoid them.

## Getting Around by Motorbike Taxis

A fast and easy way to cover short distances is the motorbike taxi; these are easily distinguished by their drivers' brightly colored vests. The taxis congregate in the island's most densely populated areas, such as Phuket Town and Patong. The cost per person starts at around B20, but negotiate a price beforehand. Wear the helmet that the driver is required by law to provide. Note that all public transport between Phuket Town and the beaches ends in the early evening, so unless you have your own wheels it's an expensive trip back.

## Getting Around by Car

If you plan to travel widely on Phuket, you might want to consider renting a car. Rates start around B1,500 per day in peak season, but are cheaper in low season. Reputable agencies, such as **Avis**, **Budget**, and **Pure Car Rent**, are located at the airport, in Phuket Town, and at the beaches. Avoid streetside operations. Valid comprehensive insurance and seat belts are mandatory, and drink-driving laws are enforced. You can also hire a car with a driver.

## Boat Trips

Long-tail boats can be chartered along the east coast to visit the islands in Phang Nga Bay, while speedboats depart from Rassada Port. Speedboats and long-tails boats can also be found on southern and west-coast beaches. The long-tail boat drivers usually post their rates on signboards, but these are usually negotiable. The cost to charter should be roughly B500 per hour.

## Getting Around by Motorbike and Bicycle

Motorbiking is a cost-effective way of seeing Phuket and allows you to travel as you please. Rentals start at around B200 per day for an automatic bike. Be cautious while riding a motorcycle here – always wear a helmet and practice defensive riding, since roads are often winding, traffic signage unreliable, and local driving skills atrocious. Give other vehicles a wide berth and expect the unexpected. If you have never ridden a motorbike before, don't start here.

Phuket is mountainous, but some areas, such as the western beaches, are ideal for easy cycling. Bicycles can be rented for about B100 per day.

## DIRECTORY

### ARRIVING BY AIR

**Air Asia**
[ 07632 8601
w airasia.com

**Bangkok Airways**
158/2–3 Yaowarat Road, Phuket Town
[ 07622 5033–5
w bangkokair.com

**Nok Air**
[ 07635 1464
w nokair.com

**Phuket International Airport**
[ E07632 7230–7
w phuketairportthai.com

**Thai Airways**
78 Ranong Road, Phuket Town [ 07636 0400
w thaiairways.com

### ARRIVING BY SEA

**Rassada Port**
Moo 1, Tambon Rassada, Muang
[ 080 535 1113
w phuketferry.com

### ARRIVING BY ROAD

**Phuket Bus Terminal 2**
Thepkrasattri Road, Ratsada, Muang
[ 07637 3193

### GETTING AROUND BY TAXI

**AOT**
w airportthai.co.th

**Grab Taxi**
w grab.com/th

### GETTING AROUND BY CAR

**Avis**
Phuket Airport
[ 089 969 8674
w avis.com

**Budget**
Phuket Airport
[ 07620 5396
w budget.co.th

**Pure Car Rent**
Phuket Airport
[ 07621 1002
w purecarrent.com

# Practical Information

## Passports and Visas

All travelers to Thailand must possess a passport valid for six months from the date of entry. Many passport holders are given tourist visa exemptions for no cost, valid for 15 days, and most Western visitors are given a 30-day tourist visa if arriving by air. For longer visits, apply at the nearest Thai embassy for a tourist visa, which must be used within three months of issue. Non-immigrant 90-day visas are available if there is a good reason for an extended stay. For a fee, 30-day visas can be extended by 10 days, and 60-day visas by 30 days at the Phuket **Immigration Office**. If you overstay your visa, there is a B500 fine per day. These regulations are subject to change, so check the **Thai Ministry of Foreign Affairs** website. Many countries, including **Australia**, the **UK**, and the **US** have consular representation in the country.

## Customs and Immigration

Travelers may bring in up to 200 cigarettes or 8 oz/ 250 g of tobacco and a liter of alcohol. Many goods purchased within Thailand qualify for a VAT refund. Look for shops with a "VAT Refund For Tourists" sign.

## Travel Safety Advice

Get up-to-date travel safety information from the **UK Foreign and Commonwealth Office**, the **US Department of State**, and the **Australian Department of Foreign Affairs and Trade**.

## Travel Insurance

Comprehensive travel insurance is essential. Medical care in Thailand is generally inexpensive, but insurance will cover any unexpectedly large claims. Keep receipts and documents to file with the insurer when you're home.

## Health

Thailand has excellent, affordable healthcare, and is a popular medical tourism destination. **Bangkok Hospital Phuket** and the **Phuket International Hospital** are the best for serious issues. For minor problems, local clinics are also hygienic and reliable, and staff generally speak the required English.

Pharmacies are usually well stocked, and prescriptions are not needed for antibiotics. Dental care is also good and inexpensive. No vaccinations are required for entering the country. While malaria is not present in Phuket, dengue fever is, so do use mosquito repellent. STDs are also a problem, and protection is essential.

## Personal Security

Crimes against visitors do take place in Phuket but you can reduce your risk. ATMs mean there's no need to carry lots of cash, and you should keep your cards in your hotel room safe. Pickpockets favor crowded areas such as street markets, and snatch thieves on motorcycles will grab a shoulder bag or purse – a day pack carried against your chest is the most secure option. Keep expensive smartphones safely out of sight.

Women should not walk alone at night or on isolated beaches, and topless sunbathing is not advised. Jet-ski operators are known to discover "damages" and insist that you pay, and the seedier sex bars are notorious for inflating checks. If you have a problem, call the **Tourist Police Hotline**.

## Currency and Banking

Thailand's currency is the baht (B), divided into 100 satang. There are B1, B2, B5, and B10 coins; notes are available for B20 (green), B50 (blue), B100 (red), B500 (purple), and B1,000 (brown).

Most banks are open 8:30am–3:30pm Monday–Friday, but branches in department stores or airports often stay open later and on weekends. ATMs are found outside bank branches, department stores, and mini-marts (although not on the smaller islands). ATMs offer an English-language option and accept major credit and debit cards, but a service charge will be applied. Cash withdrawal against credit cards can also be done in banks if the ATM won't accept your card. **Western Union** and **Moneygram** offer cash transfers from abroad, but charge high fees. Visa and MasterCard credit and debit cards are accepted by all major banks, department stores (which can apply a hefty charge), travel agents, hotels, and many restaurants. Diners Club and American Express are not widely accepted.

## Telephone and Internet

Thailand's country code is 066. When calling from abroad, omit the first 0 in the region code. Within Thailand there is no need for the country code, but you must dial the first 0 in the region code before the rest of the number.

If you own a GSM cell phone and international roaming is activated, it is easy to make and receive calls, but roaming charges can be high. Alternatively, you can buy a local SIM card in any store selling cell phones. Mobile data speeds are good, and Wi-Fi is available in hotels and restaurants, although speeds may not be high.

## Postal Services

Post office hours are normally 8:30am–4:30pm Monday–Friday and 9am–noon on Saturday. Letters to or from Europe or the US usually take a week or longer to arrive. Post offices also offer packing services. For important documents, use the **Express Mail Service (EMS)** or register the letter for an extra fee. Courier companies such as **Fedex** and **DHL** are reliable, but also expensive.

## TV, Radio, and Newspapers

Most hotel room TVs offer CNN or the BBC. Thai TV stations broadcast local and international news, while many hotels provide weather forecasts, news of upcoming events, and local features on their in-house programming.

**Phuket FM Radio** is the island's English-language radio station, with local news, popular music, and weather updates. It also streams live online.

The English-language newspaper, *Phuket Gazette*, has a good website with news and events. The weekly print version is easy to find, as is the *Bangkok Post*. Foreign newspapers are available in Phuket, but they are not always current.

## DIRECTORY

### PASSPORTS AND VISAS

**Australian Consulate-General, Phuket**
MAP K2 ■ 77/77 Chalermprakiat Rama 9 Road ( 0763 17700
w phuket.consulate.gov.au

**Immigration Office**
MAP Q6 ■ 482 Phuket Road, Phuket Town
w phuketimmigration.go.th

**Thai Ministry of Foreign Affairs**
w mfa.go.th

**UK Embassy, Bangkok**
14 Wireless Road
( 07661 5862 (honorary consulate, Phuket)
w ukinthailand.fco.gov.uk

**US Embassy, Bangkok**
95 Wireless Road
w th.usembassy.gov

### TRAVEL SAFETY ADVICE

**Australian Department of Foreign Affairs and Trade**
w dfat.gov.au
w smartraveller.gov.au

**UK Foreign and Commonwealth Office**
w gov.uk/foreign-travel-advice

**US Department of State**
w travel.state.gov

### HEALTH

**Bangkok Hospital Phuket**
MAP K2 ■ Soi Hongyok Utis, Phuket Town ( 07625 4425
w phukethospital.com

**Phuket International Hospital**
MAP K2 ■ 44 Chalermprakiat Ror 9 Road ( 07624 9400
w phuketinternationalhospital.com

### PERSONAL SECURITY

**Tourist Police Hotline**
( 1155

### CURRENCY AND BANKING

**Moneygram**
w moneygram.com

**Western Union**
w westernunion.com

### POSTAL SERVICES

**DHL**
w dhl.com

**Express Mail Service (EMS)**
w ems.post

**Fedex**
w fedex.com

### TV, RADIO, AND NEWSPAPERS

**Bangkok Post**
w bangkokpost.com

**Phuket FM Radio**
91.5–92.75FM
w phuketfmradio.com

**Phuket Gazette**
w phuketgazette.net

## Opening Hours

Stores generally open at 10am and close at 9pm or 10pm. Government offices are open 8:30am–4:30pm, but many close for lunch. Tourist attractions tend to open 9am–5pm, unless an evening program is on offer. Banks usually work 8:30am–3:30pm, but mini-branches offering money exchange are open later. Post offices work 8:30am–4:30pm Monday–Friday and 9am–noon on Saturday. On public holidays government offices, banks, and post offices are closed, but most stores remain open.

## Time Difference

Thailand is three hours behind Australian Eastern Standard Time, seven hours ahead of GMT, and 11 hours ahead of US Eastern Standard Time. Daylight saving time is not followed here.

## Electrical Appliances

Electricity in Thailand is 220 volts 50 Hz AC. Wall sockets are of the two-pin variety, and many are designed for US-style flat prongs as well as Asian-style round prongs. Irish, Australasian, and British devices will need a plug adaptor; North American devices will need both an adaptor and a converter. Both can be readily purchased on Phuket.

## Weather

Winter temperatures peak at 86° F (30° C), rising as high as 98° F (37° C) in April and May. During the rainy season from June to October temperatures are milder. Even in September and October, when rainfall is at its heaviest, Phuket still gets plenty of sunshine, but this is considered low season so hotel rates fall.

Loose, breathable clothing is best, and layering a long-sleeve top over a T-shirt is ideal, since it also offers good sun protection.

## Travelers with Disabilities

Thailand is improving wheelchair accessibility, with many hotels and department stores providing ramps and elevators. Phuket's sidewalks, however, are not wheelchair-friendly. What the island lacks in infrastructure for the disabled is made up by the helpful nature of the people. Specialized tour agencies cater to those with specific needs. **Accessible Thailand** can provide more information.

## Sources of Information

The **Tourism Authority of Thailand** has a good office in Phuket Town, with maps, brochures, and staff who can answer specific queries. Their website offers detailed information on destinations and events throughout Thailand.

Visitor centers at Khao Phra Thaeo Royal Forest and Wildlife Reserve (see pp20–21), Sirinat National Park (see pp22–3), and Khao Sok National Park (see pp32–5) offer maps, guides, and other useful services. The **Department of National Parks** has a website with useful information on planning trips, including reserving park accommodations.

Several commercial websites provide up-to-date reviews of attractions in Phuket. One of the best of these, **Phuket.com**, is a mine of information about the island's beaches, restaurants, and nightlife. For more candid and personal views, **Jamie's Phuket Blog** and **Phuket 101** are both written by long-term resident expats.

## Trips and Tours

Both scuba diving and snorkeling are popular on Phuket. **Scuba Cat Diving** offers day excursions and live-aboard boats visiting popular dive sites, such as the Similan Islands.

Cycling trips tour some of Phuket's loveliest back roads, and are a great way to experience local life. **Amazing Bike Tours Thailand** (see p55) offer trips to Khao Lak and Khao Sok National Park.

Sailing enthusiasts come here for the annual Bay Regatta and King's Cup Regatta, but Phuket is a year-round magnet for visitors who want to explore this lovely region from the water. Charter companies and yacht clubs such as **Phuket Sail Tours** offer visitors day trips and overnight tours. You could also explore the lagoons of Phang Nga Bay by kayak. **John Gray's Sea Canoe** (see p37) runs trips to aquatic grottoes, and their overnight trips include camping out on an uninhabited island. Other tours explore the mangrove forests along Phuket's coasts.

Learning to cook Thai food is a great skill to take home after your holiday, and cooking schools abound on the island. The **Blue Elephant Cooking School** begins with a visit to the market, followed by preparing, cooking, and eating your creations.

## Where to Eat

There's a wide choice of food on offer in Phuket, both in terms of price and type. You can enjoy everything from authentic Thai and fusion food to classic French, Italian, and Indian. Thai street food enjoys a reputation as one of the most delicious in the world. It's spicy, sour, tangy, and sweet, and often prepared in just a few minutes. To top it all, it is incredibly cheap and very hygienic. Eat where you see locals eating.

Another option to dine in is the food courts in shopping malls. Individual vendors (who often have their own restaurants elsewhere) offer their specialties, and you can choose selections from different stalls. Payment is usually by coupon, bought at a central kiosk.

Thai food is best shared by two or more people, with each person getting his or her own plate of rice. This allows diners to sample many different flavors and textures. Thai salads and soups are usually eaten along with main dishes, a bite of one, then a bite of the other.

Many Thai restaurants in the West tend to highlight vegetarian options, but dishes in Thailand generally include some sort of meat and are made with fish sauce. However, vegetarian food is usually available on request.

More expensive places add a service charge of 10 per cent, while some add 7 per cent for VAT as well. If no charges are added, 10 per cent is plenty.

Thais love children, so don't be surprised if the waitress wants to feed your toddler. Kid's seats are available in most restaurants, and some have children's menus.

## Where to Stay

In Phuket, the variety of accommodations range from privately-rented villas of incredible luxury to dorm rooms. Patong's simple hostels suit its nightlife-lovers, while the Cherngtalay area is for 5-star resorts. Kata offers the mid-priced beach option; the far north is for nature-seekers. It's even possible to stay in a tent on Mai Khao beach in the Sirinat National Park. Staying inland is cheaper and quieter, but you need your own transportation to reach the beach.

Although Phuket can be visited year-round, prices rise during Christmas and New Year. The high tourist season, when prices are higher and rooms should be reserved in advance, is between November and May. During the low season between June and October you should ask about reduced tariffs at hotels. Many post their rates on their websites. Accommodation booking websites such as **Agoda** and **Booking.com** are the best way to survey what's available during your intended travel dates. **Airbnb** is also very useful, especially if you prefer self-catering. It offers everything from villas to rooms in homes. Note that some of the listings are in fact public hotels. If this is the case, check for the best price offered on other booking websites.

### DIRECTORY

### TRAVELERS WITH DISABILITIES

**Accessible Thailand**
🌐 accessiblethailand.com

### SOURCES OF INFORMATION

**Department of National Parks**
🌐 park.dnp.go.th

**Jamie's Phuket Blog**
🌐 jamiesphuket.com

**Phuket 101**
🌐 phuket101.net

**Phuket.com**
🌐 phuket.com

**Tourism Authority of Thailand**
MAP P5 ■ 191 Thalang Road, Phuket Town
📞 07621 1036
🌐 tourismthailand.org

### TRIPS AND TOURS

**Blue Elephant Cooking School**
📞 07635 4355
🌐 blueelephant cookingschool.com

**Phuket Sail Tours**
📞 087 897 0492
🌐 phuketsailtours.com

**Scuba Cat Diving**
📞 07629 3120
🌐 scubacat.com

### WHERE TO STAY

**Agoda**
🌐 agoda.com

**Airbnb**
🌐 airbnb.com

**Booking.com**
🌐 booking.com

# Places to Stay

**PRICE CATEGORIES**

For a standard, double room per night (with breakfast if included), taxes, and extra charges.

**B** under B3,000 **BB** B3,000–6,000 **BBB** over B6,000

## Luxury Hotels

### Dusit Thani Laguna Phuket

MAP B6 ■ 390/1 Moo 1, Srisoonthorn Road, Cherngtalay ■ 07636 2999 ■ www.dusit.com ■ BB

Located in the Laguna Phuket Resort complex, this hotel is set in tropical gardens fronting onto the lovely Bang Tao Beach. It offers its guests access to numerous Laguna facilities, including an 18-hole golf course.

### JW Marriott Phuket Resort & Spa

MAP B2 ■ 231 Moo 3, Mai Khao Beach ■ 07633 8000 ■ www.marriott. com ■ BB

Rated as one of Asia's top luxury resorts, the Phuket Marriott was among the first high-end properties to be developed along the island's northwest coast. The guest rooms feature wooden floors, silks, and plush bedding.

### Sala Phuket Resort & Spa

MAP B2 ■ M333 Moo 3, Mai Khao Beach ■ 07633 8888 ■ www.salaresorts. com ■ BB

This ultrastylish boutique resort on Mai Khao Beach is set in gorgeous natural surroundings with five-star facilities. The design marries a classic Phuket architectural style with all modern conveniences.

## Amanpuri

MAP A6 ■ Pansea Beach ■ 07632 4333 ■ www. amanresorts.com ■ BBB

Graceful, traditional Thai architecture harmonizes with the magnificent tropical surroundings at this luxurious resort. Villas come in Thai-style pavilions, pool pavilions, and villa homes. Located on the exclusive Pansea Beach, Amanpuri has five top-rated restaurants, including the French-Japanese Naoki, which is open November to April.

### Anantara Mai Khao Phuket Villas

MAP B2 ■ 888 Moo 3, Mai Khao Beach ■ 07633 6100 ■ www.phuket.anantara. com ■ BBB

High levels of privacy and comfort await at these private villas. Rooms feature sliding glass doors that open directly onto your own private swimming pool, while tall fences and greenery guarantee maximum seclusion.

### The Sarojin

MAP F2 ■ 60 Moo 2 Kukkak, Takuapa, Phang Nga ■ 076 4279 004 ■ www.sarojin.com ■ BBB

Developed in an Asian design style, this luxury resort boasts 56 guest residences. Sheltered by Pakarang Cape, a coral headland, the resort's lovely beach offers calm swimming conditions all the year round. For the ultimate in romance, book a private dinner for two by a candlelit waterfall.

### Six Senses Yao Noi

MAP F3 ■ 56 Moo 5, Ko Yao Noi ■ 07641 8500 ■ www.sixsenses.com ■ BBB

Located on a picturesque island in Phang Nga Bay, this luxury hideaway features lush tropical gardens. Each of the resorts's 54 sumptuous villas has its own pool. The resort also offers a range of excursions and activities.

### Sri Panwa

MAP K5 ■ 31/17 Moo 8, Sakdidej Road ■ 07637 1000–3 ■ www.sripanwa. com ■ BBB

With breathtaking views from atop Panwa Cape, on the southeast coast of Phuket, Sri Panwa's villas are set amid lush tropical surroundings. They are designed in a contemporary tropical style and many of the rooms feature 360-degree views.

### The Surin Phuket

MAP A6 ■ 118 Moo 3, Pansea Beach ■ 07662 1580 ■ www.thesurin phuket.com ■ BBB

This luxury resort boasts 108 well-designed suites and cottages scattered around the beach, pool, and coconut groves. The cottages have handcrafted teakwood floors, private verandas, and secluded sun decks. Located on Pansea Bay, in the upscale Cherngtalay area, the Surin Phuket enjoys spectacular views.

### Zeavola

MAP L4 ▪ Moo 8 Laem Tong, Ko Phi Phi ▪ 07562 7000 ▪ www.zeavola. com ▪ BBB

This luxury resort is situated on Ko Phi Phi Don's northern tip. The resort's 53 guest bunga- lows are fashioned out of rich Thai teakwood, and the beds feature cool linens. The resort offers a speedboat transfer service from Phuket.

## Boutique Hotels

### Baan Yin Dee

MAP N2 ▪ 7/5 Muean Ngen Road, Patong Beach ▪ 07629 4103–6 ▪ www.baanyindee.com ▪ BB

This resort has Thai-style architecture and decora- tive finishes. On a hill above Patong, the rooftop terrace has great views and benefits from a breeze, while the pools are perfect for a cool dip. Rooms feature wooden floors and gentle lighting.

### Chanalai Flora Resort

MAP H5 ▪ 175 Koktanode Road, Kata Beach ▪ 07633 0148 ▪ www.chanalai. com ▪ BB

A modern-style resort hotel located just five minutes from the beach. The rooms are spacious, and most have balconies. The resort has two swimming pools and also provides free Wi-Fi.

### Impiana Resort Phuket

MAP N2 ▪ 41 Thaweewong Road, Patong Beach ▪ 07634 0138 ▪ www. impiana.com ▪ BB

This seaside resort enjoys access to the area's night- life venues, fine eateries, and attractions. But when you want to retire some- where peaceful, the gates to this resort transport you into a true oasis.

### The Nai Harn

MAP H5 ▪ 23/3 Vises Road, Naiharn Beach ▪ 07638 0200 ▪ www. thenaiharn.com ▪ BB

The views of Naiharn Bay from this beachfront property are breathtaking, and it is also the only hotel with direct access to the beach. The rooftop pool bar, Reflections, offers 360-degree views.

### The Old Phuket

MAP H4 ▪ 192/36 Karon Road, Karon ▪ 07639 6353–6 ▪ www.theold phuket.com ▪ BB

Designed in the classic Phuket architectural style that was popular on the island in the 19th century, this charming hotel still retains the glory of the island's tin-mining days. The rooms are modern, with clean lines; some have private Jacuzzis.

### Aleenta Resort & Spa

MAP E2 ▪ 33 Moo 5, Kok Klooy, Takuatung, Phang Nga ▪ 07658 0333 ▪ www.aleenta.com/ phuket ▪ BBB

Located 20 minutes north of Phuket airport, Aleenta offers bright and airy rooms. For the ultimate in exclusivity, book a beach- front villa, which comes with a personal butler.

### Keemala

MAP G1 ▪ Nakasud Road, Kamala ▪ 07635 8777 ▪ www.keemala.com ▪ BBB

Nestled in an old-growth forest hillside, set above Kamala Bay, each of the 38 villas has a different character, from tree houses to safari tents to thatched-roof pavilions, all done with imagination and sophistication. The ethos is wellness, with healthy food, a superb spa and yoga classes.

### Malisa Villa Suites

MAP H5 ▪ 40/36 Kata Road, Kata Beach ▪ 07628 4760-4 ▪ www.malisa villas.com ▪ BBB

The resort's name derives from the Thai word for jasmine. The rooms, designed to evoke the comforts of home with modern kitchens and comfortable living spaces, open onto private pools.

### Paresa Resort

MAP G1 ▪ 49 Moo 6, Layi- Nakalay Road, Kamala ▪ 07630 2000 ▪ www. paresaresorts.com ▪ BBB

Paresa is perched atop a cliff overlooking the Andaman Sea, between Patong and Kamala bays and surrounded by trees and flowers. This secluded boutique resort features spacious villas, many with private pools.

### Phi Phi Island Village Beach Resort

MAP F3 ▪ 97/197–9 Moo 4, Virat Hongyok Road, Ko Phi Phi ▪ 07562 8900 ▪ www.phiphiisland village.com ▪ BBB

The villas and thatched roof bungalows of this resort blend well with Ko Phi Phi Don's tropical terrain. Interiors boast rich teakwood and com- fortable luxury furnishings. The resort also has its own private beach, as well as a pool overlooking Lo Ba Goa Bay and the Andaman Sea.

### Twinpalms Phuket

MAP A6 ■ 106/46 Moo 3, Surin Beach Road ■ 07631 6500 ■ www.twinpalms-phuket.com ■ BBB

The sleek, minimalist rooms at Twinpalms are personalized with local decorative touches and bespoke furniture. The grounds feature tranquil and imaginative tropical water gardens.

## Romantic Hotels

### Cape Panwa Hotel

MAP K5 ■ 27 Moo 8, Sakdidej Road, Cape Panwa ■ 07637 2400 ■ www.capepanwa.com ■ BB

A charming property on Phuket's southeastern coast, this hotel has hosted many Hollywood film stars, while the classic Panwa House, now a restaurant, is regularly featured in movies. The hotel also has a spa, as well as access to a private beach.

### Sawasdee Village Resort and Spa

MAP H5 ■ 38 Katekwan Road, Kata Beach ■ 07633 0979 ■ www.phuket sawasdee.com ■ BB

Designed to resemble a traditional Thai village, using teakwood and Thai art and artifacts, this has been named one of the most beautiful resorts in the country.

### Andara Resort and Villas

MAP G1 ■ 15 Moo 6, Kamala ■ 07633 8777 ■www.andaraphuket. com ■ BBB

Set on a gently sloping hillside overlooking the Andaman Sea, this luxury Thai-inspired retreat boasts spacious and luxurious villas and suites, with sea views and private infinity pools. Andara Resort's restaurant, Silk *(see p66)*, serves the finest Thai cuisine in stylish surroundings.

### Banyan Tree

MAP B6 ■ 33/27 Moo 4, Srisoonthorn Road, Cherngtalay ■ 07632 4374 ■ www.banyantree. com ■ BBB

Located in the upscale Laguna resorts complex, this marvelous resort exudes romance and charm. Guests of the hotel can opt to take a dinner cruise on *Sanya Rak* ("promise of love"), an aptly named vessel for experiencing Phuket's legendary sunset.

### JW Marriott Khao Lak Resort & Spa

MAP E1 ■ 41/12 Moo 3, Khuk Khak, Takua Pa, Phang Nga ■ 07658 4888 ■ www.marriott.com ■ BBB

A popular destination for honeymooners, this beachfront resort north of Phuket island features Southeast Asia's longest swimming pool. Nearby attractions include parks, waterfalls, and scuba diving sites.

### Mom Tri's Villa Royale Phuket

MAP H5 ■ 12 Kata Noi Road, Kata Noi Beach ■ 07633 3568 ■ www. villaroyalephuket.com ■ BBB

This boutique hotel, a former royal summer house, features luxurious suites decorated with traditional Thai artistic touches. One of its three pools is carved into the seashore rocks and filled with seawater. The property's private cruiser, *Yacht Royale*, provides exclusive day trips to Phang Nga Bay.

### The Pavilions Phuket

MAP B6 ■ 31/1 Moo 6, Cherngtalay ■ 07631 7600 ■ www.thepavilions resorts.com ■ BBB

The romantic villas at this resort offer either ocean or hillside views, with unequaled privacy. Rooms all have modern Asian interiors with European touches. It also has facilities for weddings.

### The Slate Phuket

MAP B4 ■ Nai Yang Beach ■ 07632 7006 ■ www.the slatephuket.com ■ BBB

This bold property uses raw timber and modern chic to stunning effect. Suites feature subtle touches of individual artistry and have gentle lighting. The villas with private pools offer the ultimate in romantic seclusion, and the spa has treatments-for-two rooms. The hotel has received numerous awards for its trend-setting design.

### Trisara Phuket Resort

MAP B6 ■ 60/1 Moo 6, Srisoonthorn Road, Cherngtalay ■ 07631 3022 ■ www.trisara.com ■ BBB

Located on a private bay and set amongst lush tropical foliage, Trisara offers 39 private pool villas and suites with an emphasis on privacy. Dedicated cooks and service staff cater to your every need.

## Mid-Range Hotels

### Baan Krating
MAP H6 ▪ 11/3 Moo 1, Wiset Road, Rawai, Ao Sane Beach ▪ 07651 0927 ▪ www.baankrating.com ▪ B

With a lush jungle setting, Baan Krating is a haven of seclusion and peace. The villas are well appointed, clean, and comfortable. The beach bar overlooks Naiharn Bay.

### Metropole Phuket
MAP P5 ▪ 1 Soi Surin, Montri Road, Phuket Town ▪ 07621 4020 ▪ www.metropolephuket.com ▪ B

The Metropole Phuket offers 248 rooms and suites in Phuket Town. Guests can enjoy traditional Thai-style spa massages, or dine at the two restaurants or in the executive cocktail lounge.

### The Royal Palm Beach Front
MAP N1 ▪ 66/2 Thaweewong Road, Patong ▪ 07634 2424 ▪ www.theroyalpalm.com ▪ B

Smart interiors define the 67 rooms at the Royal Palm, located in the heart of Patong. With a range of facilities, including an outdoor pool and Jacuzzi, a steam room, and a spa, the hotel offers travelers many comforts.

### Sino House
MAP P5 ▪ 1 Montri Rd., Phuket Town ▪ 076 232 494 ▪ www.sinohouse phuket.com ▪ B

Sino House is a modern three story building, near the Old Town area, nicely decorated and furnished in Sino-Portuguese style. Rooms are large and airy, with floor-to-ceiling windows overlooking a pretty garden.

### Baan Laimai Beach Resort
MAP N1 ▪ 66 Thaweewong Road, Patong ▪ 07634 2620 ▪ www.baanlaimai.com ▪ BB

This resort offers privacy in the heart of Patong. Some rooms feature hardwood floors and Asian-inspired design. The swimming pool encircles an island with palm trees, accessed via a charming bridge.

### Kamala Beach Resort
MAP G1 ▪ 96/42–3, Moo 3, Kamala Beach, Kathu, Phuket ▪ 07634 2620 ▪ www.kamalabeach.com ▪ BB

Located close to the beach, the weekend market, and good restaurants, the Kamala Beach Resort has four pools, a massage parlour, and a gym. Guests must be over 16 years of age.

### Kata Palm Resort and Spa
MAP H5 ▪ 60 Kata Road, Kata ▪ 07628 4334 ▪ www.katapalmresort.com ▪ BB

The comfortable rooms are furnished in Thai wood and fabrics, with hand-carved teak decorations. With Karon and Kata nearby, guests are close to great shopping, dining, and nightlife.

### Manathai Surin
MAP A6 ▪ 121 Srisoonthorn Road, Surin ▪ 07627 0900–5 ▪ www.manathai.com ▪ BB

A stylish boutique hotel on Surin Beach, Manathai blends contemporary architectural design with classic Asian styles, textures, and fabrics. The spa offers a range of therapeutic massages, scrubs, and wraps.

### Millennium Resort
MAP N2 ▪ 199 Rat Uthit 200 Pee Road, Patong ▪ 07660 1999 ▪ www.millenniumhotels.com ▪ BB

Located off the beach in Patong, this resort gets high marks from visitors for its location. It is next to the upscale Jungceylon shopping mall, and also surrounded by popular restaurants and vibrant nightlife. Rooms range from simple chic studios to expansive suites.

### Burasari Patong Boutique Hotel
MAP N2 ▪ 18/110 Ruamjai Road, Patong ▪ 07629 2929 ▪ www.burasari.com ▪ BBB

Named after the rare flower that blooms on the property, this hotel offers tranquility and rooms decorated in an elegant classic northern Thai Lanna (traditional style) fashion.

### Mangosteen Resort & Spa
MAP J5 ▪ 99/4 Moo 7, Soi Mangosteen, Rawai ▪ 07628 9399 ▪ www.mangosteen-phuket.com ▪ BBB

A peaceful hilltop resort, the Mangosteen enjoys lovely views of the hills, beaches, and bays of Phuket. At night there's a free shuttle service to the nearby Rawai and Naiharn beaches.

*For a key to hotel price categories see p112*

## Budget Hotels

### Andatel Hotel Patong Phuket
MAP N2 ▪ 41/9 Rat Uthit 200 Pee Road, Patong ▪ 07629 0480 ▪ www. andatelhotel.com ▪ B

A short distance from the beach, this hotel has classic Thai-style villas and a charming pool that receives sunlight through the day. Rooms are simple but well kept.

### Deevana Patong Resort & Spa
MAP N2 ▪ 43/2 Rat Uthit, 200 Pee Road, Patong ▪ 07634 1414–5 ▪ www. deevanapatong.com ▪ B

This secluded 4-star resort, surrounded by tropical gardens, sprawls across 12 acres (5 ha) of land in Patong. On your doorstep, however, are the island's best nightlife, fine dining, and entertainment venues. Simple, clean guest rooms are tastefully decorated and quite comfortable.

### Good 9 @ Home
MAP H6 ▪ Soi Wassana, Viset Road, Rawai ▪ 081 834 3898 ▪ www.face book.com/good9athome ▪ B

A simple, seven-room guesthouse, this gets great reviews for cleanliness and friendly staff. The location is very quiet, yet just a few minutes' walk from Rawai Beach. Do book in advance.

### Hemingway's Hotel
MAP N3 ▪ 188/17–20 Phangmuang, Patong ▪ 07654 0895 ▪ www. hemingwayshotel.com ▪ B

The name of this hotel evokes images of exotic destinations populated by larger-than-life literary characters. The rooms boast rich wood paneling and furniture, lush silk throws and pillows, and tranquil Buddha images. The hotel is good value for money in Patong.

### Kata Beach Studio
MAP H4 ▪ 90/5 Khoktanod Road, Kata ▪ 07633 3323 ▪ www. katabeachstudio.com ▪ B

Guests can really make themselves at home in these modern studios, which boast kitchens and balconies. The rooftop pool and Jacuzzi benefit from impressive views. There is also a swanky poolside bar that is open daily until 10pm.

### The Memory at On On Hotel
MAP K3 ▪ 19 Phang Nga Road, Phuket Town ▪ 07621 1154 ▪ B

Phuket Town's oldest hotel, although recently and tastefully renovated, still retains a special character and charm. Budget-price dorm rooms have curtains for privacy. If it looks familiar, a scene from the movie *The Beach* was filmed here.

### Nai Yang Beach Resort
MAP B3 ▪ 65/23–4 Nai Yang Beach Road ▪ 07632 8300 ▪ B

Located in the heart of Sirinat National Park, the resort promises a relaxing stay at prices that are tough to beat. The scenery is memorable – you drive past a rubber plantation on the way, and the resort is set right on Nai Yang Beach.

### Patong Pearl Resortel
MAP N1 ▪ 3 Sawadirak Road, Patong ▪ 07634 0121 ▪ B

With its central location in Patong, this modern and well-maintained hotel is a comfortable place at which to unwind in the middle of the busy city. A swimming pool and sun deck lift the Patong Pearl a cut above other budget properties.

### Rattana Beach Hotel
MAP H4 ▪ 72/2–5 Patak Road, Karon ▪ 07639 6415–7 ▪ B

The Rattana offers guests well-priced accommodations close to Karon Beach. Superior rooms have balconies overlooking the pool. Enjoy a cocktail at the poolside bar, or a short stroll to the beach.

### White Sand Resortel
MAP N1 ▪ 3–7 Sawadirak Road, Patong ▪ 07629 6013–8 ▪ www.whitesand patong.com ▪ B

Quiet rooms and very spacious suites all come with a private balcony and sea or garden views. The hotel restaurant is well known for its fresh seafood, and there's a rooftop pool.

## Family Hotels

### Hilton Phuket Arcadia Resort & Spa
MAP H4 ▪ 333 Patak Road, Karon ▪ 07639 6433 ▪ www.hilton.com ▪ BB

This is a vast, tropical garden complex on Karon beach, with multiple pools and tennis and squash courts, as well as a choice of ten restaurants. There is also a Kidz Paradise club, with a team of professionals to keep the children happy while parents are enjoying the spa, gym, or beach.

### Holiday Inn Resort Phuket

MAP N2 ■ 52 Thaweewong Road, Patong ■ 07637 0200 ■ phuket.holidayinn resorts.com ■ BB

With specially designed family and kids' suites, this resort also has an extensive Kids Club for children under 12. Club 12, a parent-free zone with Internet, games, movies, and karaoke, is perfect for teenagers.

### Laguna Holiday Club Resort

MAP B6 ■ 61 Moo 4, Srisoonthorn Road, Cherngtalay ■ 07627 1888 ■ www.laguna holidayclubresort.com ■ BB

An all-suite resort, this is the most kid-friendly option in the sedate Laguna area. The Kids Club organizes painting and mask-making events, treasure hunts, bowling, and an introduction to Thai games and crafts. Kids over eight can take scuba lessons; babysitting facilities are available.

### Phuket Graceland Resort & Spa

MAP N1 ■ 190 Thaweewong Road, Patong ■ 07637 0500 ■ www.phuketgraceland. com ■ BB

The Graceland Resort's Kids Club gives children a supervised place in which to play and watch movies. There is also a bowling alley, swimming pool, and a Jacuzzi.

### Angsana Laguna Phuket

MAP B6 ■ Srisoonthorn Road, Cherngtalay ■ 07635 8500 ■ www. angsana.com ■ BBB

Aside from the expansive grounds (perfect for cycling) and the ocean- and lagoon-based water sports (sailing and paddle boarding), the Angsana's Tree House Kids Club gets top reviews. Even the spa has a specially tailored children's menu.

### Katathani Phuket Beach Resort

MAP H4 ■ 14 Kata Noi Road, Karon Beach ■ 07633 0009 ■ www. katathani.com ■ BBB

Situated on the secluded Kata Noi Bay, this stylish, self-contained luxury beach resort features six outdoor swimming pools, including four specially for kids, sports and crafts classes, a Kids Club, and six restaurants.

### Le Meridien Phuket Beach Resort

MAP H4 ■ 29 Soi Karon Nui, Karon ■ 07637 0100 ■ www.starwoodhotels. com ■ BBB

This resort's Penguin Club for kids aged 3–12 years offers a range of activities. The resort features a mini-golf course, rock-climbing wall, and multiple pools. Children can also learn Thai dancing, cartoon drawing, and how to make ice cream.

### Metadee Resort

MAP H4 ■ 66 Kata Road, Kata ■ 07633 7888 ■ www.metadee phuket. com ■ BBB

Near Kata Yai Beach, this chic resort has rooms in a unique setting – they are in a garden surrounded by a large pool. As a result, nearly every room enjoys direct access to the water. There is also a special children's pool and a fitness center.

### Mövenpick Resort & Spa

MAP H4 ■ 509 Patak Road, Karon ■ 07639 6139 ■ www.moeven pick-hotels.com ■ BBB

The resort's Play Zone is one of the largest on Phuket. Here, children can participate in a variety of supervised activities.

### Outrigger Laguna Phuket Beach Resort

MAP B6 ■ 323 Moo 2, Srisoonthorn, Bang Tao ■ 07636 0600 ■ www. outriggerthailand.com ■ BBB

Offering a park with pools, a waterslide, and a range of other activities from kayaking to water basketball, this resort is perfect for families. The Kids Club also puts on a roster of daily events to suit their younger guests.

### Renaissance Phuket Resort & Spa

MAP B2 ■ 555 Moo 3, Mai Khao Beach ■ 07636 3999 ■ www.marriott.com ■ BBB

Surrounded by greenery and featuring a water-slide, the kids' pool at this resort is a favorite. Away from the water, the Kids Club entertains youngsters with movies, puzzles, books, and video games, all supervised by childcare professionals. The lovely grounds are set within a national park.

*For a key to hotel price categories see p112*

# General Index

# Acknowledgments

## Author

A frequent traveler to Phuket and southern Thailand, William Bredesen has been the assistant editor of *Bangkok Post The Magazine* since 2009. He has previously worked on a contemporary Thai history book, *Chronicle of Thailand: Headline News Since 1946*, and he holds a Master's degree in Southeast Asian Studies from Chulalongkorn University in Bangkok.

**Additional Contributor** Peter Holmshaw

**Publishing Director** Georgina Dee

**Publisher** Vivien Antwi

**Design Director** Phil Ormerod

**Editorial** Sophie Adam, Ankita Awasthi Tröger, Michelle Crane, Rebecca Flynn, Rachel Fox, Akshay Rana, Sally Schafer, Sands Publishing Solutions

**Cover Design** Richard Czapnik

**Design** Tessa Bindloss, Bharti Karakoti, Vinita Venugopal

**Picture Research** Susie Peachey, Ellen Root, Lucy Sienkowska

**Commissioned Photography** Brent Madison

**Cartography** Subhashree Bharti, Suresh Kumar, Stuart James, Casper Morris

Base mapping supplied by Huber Kartographie

**DTP** Jason Little

**Production** Jude Crozier

**Factchecker** Neil Ray

**Proofreader** Clare Peel

**Indexer** Hilary Bird

## Picture Credits

The publisher would like to thank the following for their kind permission to reproduce their photographs:
**Key:** a-above; b-below/bottom; c-centre; f-far; l-left; r-right; t-top

**123RF.com:** Sergey Belov 76-7; Nilanjan Bhattacharya 77cr; John Hu 74b; milxela 69tl; Patryk Kośmider 100-1; Chirasak Tolertmongkol 20clb.

**Alamy Stock Photo:** age fotostock / Gonzalo Azumendi 65cl; allOver images 1; Mary Andrews 84b; Arco Images / Kiedrowski; R. 71tr; Arco Images GmbH / K. Kreder 4cl, 57cl; David Austin 28br; Sergey Belov 4b; Chronicle 41tr; Sorin Colac 36-7; Danita Delimont / Stuart Westmorland 11cr; Gary Dublanko 36cl; Eagle Visions Photography / Craig Lovell

11cb; Chris Fredriksson 82b; Robert Fried 71cl; Kevin Hellon 3tr, 15cra, 92-3, 104-5; Friedrich von Hörsten 30br; imageBROKER / Stella 23tl, 27tl; International Photobank 74tc; Kees Metselaar 91t; Jason Knott 12cl, 53cl, 68cla; LOOK Die Bildagentur der Fotografen GmbH / Thomas Stankiewicz 19bl; Craig Lovell 52c; Benny Marty 4t; MediaWorldImages 4clb; MO:SES 4crb; National Geographic Creative 94tr; Ernita Nenggala 54clb; Panther Media GmbH / perszing1982 2tl, 8-9; parasola.net 48-9, 98tl; Dmitry Rukhlenko - Travel Photos 7br; M. Sobreira 2tr, 38-9, 53br; Samuel Spicer 32clb; travelstock44.de / Juergen Held 48cla; Peter Treanor 19crb; Peter Vallance 22cl; Steve Vidler 54-5; Matthew Wakem 55tr; Jan Wlodarczyk 44-5; Andrew Woodley 63c; Zoonar GmbH / Sergey Pristyazhnyuk (Serg Zastavkin) 26crb.

**Banyan Tree Gallery Phuket:** 95cr.

**Black Ginger:** 97cr.

**Bridgeman Images:** History / Rainer Krack 40t.

**Dreamstime.com:** Dimitris Apostolou 28-9; Stuart Atkinson 42bc; Babycoconut 14bl; Ihar Balaikin 82tl; Banky405 11tr; Sergey Belov 35b; Pipop Boosarakumwadi 6cla; Mr. Phonlawat Chaicheevinlikit 60br; Pakphipat Charoenrach 10cr; Doraclub 23br; Jakob Fischer 76crb; Fabio Formaggio 65tr; Geargodz 96t; Sean Harms 16-7; Jaroon Ittiwannapong 73cl; Attila Jandi 35cra; Jedynakanna 102br; Kajornyot 34cr; Sombat Khamin 12-3, 42t; Khellon 11br, 12br, 14t; Kogolffoto 88-9; Patryk Kosmider 33tl; Torsten Kuenzlen 92clb; Ratchanikon Kulaptip 52t; Manit Larpluechai 33crb; Adam Laws 11ca; Chee-onn Leong 10br; Lestor 49cl; Jedsada Luadthainarong 13cr; Thanawut Makawan 18-9; Maria Malkina 26cla; Aliaksandr Mazurkevich 17br; Sophie Mcaulay 70crb; Mosaymay 10cla; Mullrich 10clb; Apidech Ninkhlai 4cla; Nokhook 75cla; Kampee Patisena 37clb; Pavantt 26-7; Alexey Pavlov 46t; Wiroj Phongthadaporn 30-1; Pakpoom Phummee 10cra, 15bl; Ppy2010ha 67tr; Viacheslav Ryukhko 23clb; Smolny1 75b; Lee Snider 18clb, 19tl, 47cr; Tayawee Supan 44tl, 68-9; Suriya007 34bl; Suttipong Sutiratanachai 99b; Tagstiles 50b; Thawats 21bl; Artit Thongchuea 32br; Tuayai 17tl; Nuttawut Uttamaharad 27cr; Valentyn75 69b; Yongkiet 3tl, 36br, 78-9; Zastavkin 29br.

**Dusit Thani Laguna Phuket:** Ton Santipong 66bl.

**FLPA:** OceanPhoto 31clb.

**Getty Images:** Pete Atkinson 77tl; Paula Bronstein 41clb; Adisorn Fineday Chutikunakorn 72b; Ashit Desai 72tl; Reinhard Dirscherl 56tl; Michael Freeman 71bl; Gallo Images / Danita Delimont 31br; John Harper 50tl; Martin Harvey 34tl; Kaveh Kazemi 46bl; Lonely Planet 21tl, 61cl; Lonely Planet Images / Paul Kennedy 29tl, / Wibowo Rusli 17cr; LOOK-foto / Ingolf Pompe 58-9; 67cl; Moment / Luciana Calvin 101cla, / Sirachai Arunrugstichai 30cl, / Vincent Jary 102cl; Moviepix / Keith Hamshere 63tr; Norbert Probst 83cl; Sebun Photo / Youjiro Oda 81tr; Iryna Shpulak 91br; simonlong 62tr; Sirachai Arunrugstichai 99tl; Ullstein Bild / Raimund Franken 56b, 73tr, 80cla; Ullstein Bild / Reinhard Dirscherl 4cra; 57tr; Stuart Westmorland 54tr.

**The Gibbon Rehabilitation Project:** 93bl.

**iStockphoto.com:** 4FR 24-5; lkunl 32-3.

**Paresa Resorts:** 87clb.

**Phuket FantaSea:** 60t.

**Rex Shutterstock:** Paul Brown 100tl.

**Robert Harding Picture Library:** Ingolf Pompe 62b; Luca Tettoni 81clb.

**SuperStock:** Hemis.fr / Julien Garcia 51tl; imageBROKER / Josef Beck 94b.

**White Box Restaurant:** Stefano Beber 66tr.

### Cover
Front and spine: **Alamy Stock Photo:** Jan Wlodarczyk

Back: **Dreamstime.com:** Edigos

### Pull Out Map Cover
**Alamy Stock Photo:** Jan Wlodarczyk

All other images © Dorling Kindersley
For further information see: www.dkimages.com

*As a guide to abbreviations in visitor information blocks: **Adm** = admission charge; **DA** = disabled access; **D** = dinner; **L** = lunch.*

Penguin
Random
House

Printed and bound in China

First published in Great Britain in 2012
by Dorling Kindersley Limited
80 Strand, London WC2R 0RL

Copyright 2012, 2017 © Dorling
Kindersley Limited

A Penguin Random House Company

17 18 19 20 10 9 8 7 6 5 4 3 2 1

**Reprinted with revisions 2014, 2017**

A CIP catalogue record is available from the British Library.

ISBN 978 0 2412 7901 4

MIX
Paper from
responsible sources
FSC™ C018179

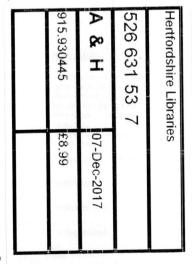

# Phrase Book

Thai is a tonal language and regarded by most linguists as head of a distinct language group, though it incorporates many Sanskrit words from ancient India, and some modern English ones, too. There are five tones: mid, high, low, rising, and falling. The particular tone, or pitch, at which each syllable is pronounced determines its meaning. For instance "mâi" (falling tone) means "not," but "mǎi" (rising tone) is "silk." See the Guidelines for Pronunciation, below, for a phonetic transliteration of the Thai script for English speakers, including guidance for tones in the form of accents.

### Guidelines for Pronunciation

When reading the phonetics, pronounce syllables as if they form English words. For instance:

| | |
|---|---|
| *a* = as in "ago" | *ay* = as in "day" |
| *e* = as in "hen" | *er* = as in "enter" |
| *i* = as in "thin" | *ew* = as in "few" |
| *o* = as in "on" | *oh* = as in "go" |
| *u* = as in "gun" | *oo* = as in "boot" |
| *ah* = as in "rather" | *OO* = as in "book" |
| *ai* = as in "Thai" | *oy* = as in "toy" |
| *air* = as in "pair" | *g* = as in "give" |
| *ao* = as in "Mao Zedong" | *ng* = as in "sing" |

These sounds have no close equivalents in English:

| | |
|---|---|
| eu | can be likened to a sound of disgust - the sound could be written as "errgh" |
| bp | a single sound between a "b" and a "p" |
| dt | a single sound between a "d" and a "t" |

Note that when "p," "t," and "k" occur at the end of Thai words, the sound is "swallowed." Also note that many Thais use an "l" instead of an "r" sound.

### The Five Tones

Accents indicate the tone of each syllable.

| | |
|---|---|
| no mark | The *mid tone* is voiced at the speaker's normal, even pitch. |
| á é í ó ú | The *high tone* is pitched slightly higher than the mid tone. |
| à è ì ò ù | The *low tone* is pitched slightly lower than the mid tone. |
| ǎ ě ǐ ǒ ǔ | The *rising tone* sounds like a questioning pitch, starting low and rising. |
| â ê î ô û | The *falling tone* sounds similar to a syllable word for emphasis. |

## In an Emergency

| | |
|---|---|
| Help! | chôo-ay dôo-ay! |
| Fire! | fai mâi! |
| Where is the nearest hospital? | tâir-o née mee rohng pa-yah-bahn yòo têe-nài? |
| Call an ambulance! | rêe-uk rót pa-yah-bahn hâi nòy! |
| Call a doctor! | rêe-uk mŏr hâi nòy! |
| Call the police! | rêe-uk dtum ròo-ut hâi nòy! |

## Communication Essentials

| | |
|---|---|
| Yes | châi or krúp/kâ |
| No | mâi châi or mâi krúp/mâi kâ |

| | |
|---|---|
| Please can you...? | chôo-ay |
| Thank you | kòrp-kOOn |
| No, thank you | mâi ao kòrp-kOOn |
| Excuse me/sorry | kŏr-tôht (krúp/kâ) |
| Hello | sa-wùt dee (krúp/kâ) |
| Goodbye | lah gòrn ná |

## Useful Phrases

| | |
|---|---|
| How are you? | kOOn sa-bai dee reu (krúp/kâ)? |
| Very well, thank you | sa-bai dee (krúp/kâ) |
| How do I get to...? | ...bpai yung-ngai? |
| Do you speak English? | kOOn pôot pah-săh ung-grit bpen mái? |
| I can't speak Thai. | pôot pah-săh tai mâi bpen |
| Where is the nearest public telephone? | tâir-o née mee toh-ra-sùp yòo têe-nài? |

## Useful Words

| | |
|---|---|
| hot | rórn |
| cold | yen or năo |
| good | dee |
| bad | mâi dee |
| open | bpèrt |
| closed | bpìt |
| left | sái |
| right | kwăh |
| near | glâi |
| toilet | hôrng náhm |

## Shopping

| | |
|---|---|
| How much does this cost? | nêe rah-kah tâo-rài? |
| Do you have? | mee...mái? |
| Do you take credit cards/traveler's checks? | rub but cray-dit/ chék dern tang mái? |
| What time do you open/close? | bpèrt/bpìt gèe mohng? |
| Can you ship this overseas? | sòng khŏng nee bpai dtàhng bpra-tâyt dâi mái? |
| Could you lower the price a bit? | lót rah-kah nòy dâi mái? |
| How about...baht? | ...bàht dâi mái? |
| I'll settle for...baht. | ...bàht gôr láir-u-gun |
| Thai silk | pâh-mǎi tai |
| pharmacy | ráhn kǎi yah |
| market | dta-làht |
| supermarket | sŎOp-bpêr-mah-gèt |

## Staying in a Hotel

| | |
|---|---|
| Do you have a vacant room? | mee hôrng wâhng mái? |
| air-conditioned room | hôrng air |
| I'd like a room for one night/three nights. | (pŏm/dee-chún) ja púk yòo keun nèung/ sǎhm keun |

| | |
|---|---|
| What is the charge per night? | kâh hôrng wun la tâo-rái? |
| May I see the room first please? | kôr doo hôrng gòrn dâi mái? |
| Will you spray some mosquito repellent, please? | chôo-ay chèet yah gun yOOng hâi nòy dâi mái? |
| double/twin room | hôrng kôo |
| single room | hôrng dèe-o |
| bill | bin |
| key | gOOn-jair |
| shower | fùk boo-a |
| swimming pool | sà wâi náhm |

## Sightseeing

| | |
|---|---|
| tourist office | sŭm-núk ngahn gahn tôrng têe-o |
| tourist police | dtum-ròo-ut tôrng têe-o |
| beach | hàht or chai-hàht |
| island (ko) | gòr |
| museum | pí-pít-ta-pun |
| national park | ÒO-ta yahn hàirng châht |
| temple (wat) | wút |
| Thai boxing | moo-ay tai |
| Thai massage | nôo-ut |
| trekking | gahn dern tahng tâo |

## Transportation

| | |
|---|---|
| How long does it take to get to...? | chái way-lah nahn tâo-rái bpai tĕung têe...? |
| What station is this? | têe nêe sa-tăhn-nee a-rai? |
| ticket | dtŏo-a |
| air-conditioned bus | rót bprùp ah-gàht |
| airport | sa-năhm bin |
| tour bus | rót too-a |
| train | rót fai |
| bus station | sa-tăhn-nee rót may |
| moped | rót mor-dter-sai |
| taxi | táirk-sêe |

## Eating Out

| | |
|---|---|
| A table for two please. | kŏr dtó sŭm-rùp sŏrng kon |
| May I see the menu? | kŏr doo may-noo nòy? |
| Do you have...? | mee...mái? |
| Is it spicy? | pèt mái? |
| May I have a glass of water, please. | kŏr núm kàirng bplào gâir-o nèung |
| Waiter/waitress! | kOOn (krúp/kâ) |
| The check, please. | kŏr bin nòy (krúp/kâ) |

## Menu Decoder

| | |
|---|---|
| néu-a woo-a | |
| bee-a | |
| yâhng | |
| gài | |
| prík | |

| | |
|---|---|
| beef | |
| beer | |
| char-grilled | |
| chicken | |
| chili | |

| | |
|---|---|
| gah-fair | coffee |
| bpoo | crab |
| mèe gròrp | crispy noodles |
| gŏo-ay dtĕe-o hâirng | dry noodles |
| bpèt | duck |
| tÓO-ree-un | durian |
| kài | egg |
| bplah | fish |
| kĭng | ginger |
| núm kàirng bplào | iced water |
| hèt | mushroom |
| gŏo-ay dtĕe-o-náhm | noodle soup |
| ma-la-gor | papaya |
| sùp-bpa-rót | pineapple |
| néu-a-mŏo | pork |
| kâo | rice |
| gŏo-ay dtĕe-o | rice noodles |
| gÔOng | shrimp |
| ah-hăhn wâhng | soy sauce |
| núm chah | tea |
| pùk | vegetables |
| náhm | water |

## Health

| | |
|---|---|
| I do not feel well | róo-sèuk mâi sa-bai |
| I have a fever | dtoo-a-rórn bpen kâi |
| asthma | rôhk hèut |
| diabetes | rôhk bao wăhn |
| diarrhea | tórng sĕe-a |
| dizzy | wee-un hŏo-a |
| stomach ache | bpòo-ut tórng |
| aspirin | air-sa-bprin or yah-gâir kâi |
| doctor | mŏr |
| dentist | tun-dta-pâirt or mŏr fun |
| hospital | rohng pa-yah-bahn |
| medicine | yah |
| prescription | bai sùng yah |
| I'm allergic to... | (pŏm/dee-chún) páir... |

## Numbers

| | |
|---|---|
| 0 | sŏon |
| 1 | nèung |
| 2 | sŏrng |
| 3 | săhm |
| 4 | sèe |
| 5 | hâh |
| 6 | hòk |
| 7 | jèt |
| 8 | bpàirt |
| 9 | gâo |
| 10 | sìp |
| 100 | nèung róy |
| 1000 | nèung pan |
| one hour | nèung chôo-a mohng |
| half an hour | krêung chôo-a mohng |
| Sunday | wun ah-tít |
| Monday | wun jun |
| Tuesday | wun ung-kahn |
| Wednesday | wun pÓOt |
| Thursday | wun pa-réu-hùt |
| Friday | wun sÒOk |
| Saturday | wun săo |

# Selected Sight Index